IN THE FINEST TRADITION

His Imperial Majesty Nicolas II, Tsar of All the Russias, in full dress uniform of a Colonel of the 2nd Dragoons (Royal Scots Greys) 1902, by Valentin Serov (1865-1911). The last Tsar was Colonel-in-Chief of the Royal Scots Greys from 1894 until 1916. By permission of the Commanding Officer, The Royal Scots Dragoon Guards (Carabiniers & Greys).

IN THE FINEST TRADITION

THE ROYAL SCOTS
DRAGOON GUARDS
(Carabiniers & Greys)

ITS HISTORY AND TREASURES

STEPHEN WOOD

Foreword
Lieutenant-Colonel
M.S. JAMESON

Preface
Lieutenant-General
SIR NORMAN ARTHUR

Copyright © Stephen Wood, 1988

First published in Great Britain in 1988 by
MAINSTREAM PUBLISHING COMPANY (EDINBURGH) LTD
7 Albany Street, Edinburgh EH1 3UG

ISBN 1 85158 174 X (cloth)

British Cataloguing in Publication Data

Wood, Stephen
   In the finest tradition: the Royal Scots
   Dragoon Guards (Carabiniers and Greys):
   its history and treasures.
   1. Great Britain. Army. Royal Scots Dragoon
   Guards, to 1988
   I. Title
   356'.11'0941

   ISBN 1-85158-174-X

Typeset in 11 on 13pt Garamond by Bookworm Typesetting, Edinburgh
Printed in Great Britain by Butler & Tanner, Frome, Somerset

DEDICATION

For all ranks of The Royal Scots Dragoon Guards,
past, present and future,
makers and guardians of the finest traditions

CONTENTS

ACKNOWLEDGEMENTS

This book is the result of the imagination of a number of officers of the Royal Scots Dragoon Guards, who felt that it should be produced. That it was ever written is due to the assiduous encouragement given me by the Commanding Officer, Lieutenant Colonel Melville Jameson, the knowledgeable enthusiasm for it of the Regiment's second-in-command, Major Henry Callander, and the helpful tolerance of the Officers and Men of the Regiment.

Singled out, invidiously, for their very special help to the author and photographer must be Major Michael Tippett, Captains Simon Hearn, Jeremy Kelton and James Melville, Regimental Sergeant-Major Brian Cullen, Mess Sergeant-Major Derek Bennett, Sergeant Colin Williams, Corporals Stanley Hynds and Iain Massie and Trooper Ian Trimby.

Thanks for willing co-operation go to Major Terry Morton and Mr Jim Hall, Home Headquarters, The Royal Scots Dragoon Guards (Carabiniers & Greys); to Major Tony Astle, Assistant Regimental Secretary, RHQ Cheshire Regiment, and to Mr Ron Ng, Museum Attendant, Chester Military Museum.

I have to thank my Director, Dr Robert Anderson, for allowing me to write this book, and would like to thank my ever-patient colleagues for their unwavering assistance, especially Allan Carswell, George Dalgleish, Godfrey Evans and June McDonald.

The undoubted talents of Mrs Joyce Smith as a photographer permeate this book since more than 95 per cent of its photographs are her work; she deserves my thanks and your admiration.

In her very limited spare time, Helen McCorry has acted as researcher, advisor and copy editor to an increasingly frantic author. She merits a high degree of praise, is largely responsible for the structure of the end result and has my sincere gratitude.

To my distinguished colleagues and friends, Colonel (E.R.) Marc Neuville and Dr Jean-Marcel Humbert of the Musée de l'Armée in Paris, I extend my thanks for their interest and their co-operation in producing a photograph of one of the few regimental treasures to have "gone away". I would also like to thank Frau Sabina Hermes of the Wehrgeschichtliches Museum, Schloss Rastatt, for her help in tracing the unwitting donor of one of the Regiment's few war trophies.

My thanks for willing co-operation go, too, to Miss Corinne Miller of Leeds City Art Gallery. Marilyn and John Hayward deserve my thanks for their rapid answer to a request for information about Abu Klea. Helen Forrest again deserves my thanks for turning manuscript into typescript.

PREFACE

By Lieutenant General Sir Norman Arthur KCB, Colonel,
The Royal Scots Dragoon Guards (Carabiniers and Greys)

The Royal Scots Dragoon Guards inherit the history and the fame of three grand old regiments. This has bestowed upon the Regiment an immensely full and colourful past – more than 300 years of service, campaigns and combat, on foot, on horse and in armour, in most continents. The Regiment is proud of this inheritance and sees itself not only as a very professional military unit but also as a close community. This community incorporates those who are serving and those who have already served and their families, as well as those cadets, sons and candidates for the Regiment who, in time, will serve. This entity has arisen from the most recent amalgamation in the British Army, an amalgamation of three of its oldest and most individual regiments. While its professional competence and its fighting equipment grow ever sharper, this very peaceable community seems to grow closer with each decade that passes.

The Regiment matches its proud history and traditions with beautiful possessions, pictures, silver and relics bestowed, captured or earned by its service through the years. It has been an inspired idea to bring the two together within the covers of what proves to be an excellent and original history book.

FOREWORD

By Lieutenant Colonel M S Jameson, Commanding Officer
The Royal Scots Dragoon Guards (Carabiniers and Greys)

This is the first complete history that has been written on The Royal Scots Dragoon Guards, Scotland's senior regiment, and only regiment of cavalry. It has been kept deliberately brief and easy to digest, yet it tells the story of the three Regiments, the 3rd Dragoon Guards, the 6th Dragoon Guards and The Royal Scots Greys, from their birth to amalgamation and the progress of the Regiment since then to this day. It contains many illustrations of the fine pictures and silver in the possession of the officers' mess, warrant officers' and sergeants' mess and corporals' mess which are well recorded in this volume and bring to life the remarkable history of the Regiment over the last 310 years.

It is the first time that our treasures have been properly recorded and for that reason alone it is a worthwhile venture. We are lucky in having the heirlooms of three famous regiments, who between them have served with distinction on most of the world's continents and in the majority of the campaigns of the eighteenth, nineteenth and twentieth centuries; we therefore guard them proudly for the generations of officers and men yet to come.

As the author of this book Stephen Wood, the Keeper of the Scottish United Services Museum, is particularly well qualified. He brings his impressive knowledge of military history as well as his familiarity with the Regiment's history, traditions and heirlooms, into play with skill and objectivity. I am most grateful to him for agreeing to write this book and particularly pleased that he has produced it in a form which I believe will provide a most useful document to those in the Regiment and the Army, and an attractive illustrated history of the Regiment to those outside. However protective we in the Regiment may feel about our treasured possessions, they do represent an important part of the history of Great Britain and it behoves us to put them on display for all to see.

From this perspective, therefore, this book should commend itself to all who are interested in military history, social history and the history of art or a combination of all three as encapsulated in this volume.

INTRODUCTION

It is now axiomatic that the regimental system of the British Army is one of its many strengths. British regiments have, rightly, been equated with ancient families, each generation drawing inspiration and support from the example of past generations and forging, sometimes remarkably rapidly, traditions that add to the qualities which predecessors provide. Thus, telling the story of a British regiment is very like telling that of a family. So, too, as when a family contracts a major marriage alliance with another family of similar age and standing, does the story broaden and become more, potentially, complicated. Families which have occupied the same house, or houses, for generations inevitably accumulate objects which reflect the family history. So, too, do regiments. Families which ally in marriage multiply their heirlooms yet, also, tend to disperse them among the ever-increasing shoots from the branches of the family tree. Regiments do not, except in the rare cases of disbandment. Thus is a history such as this illustrated: with the accumulated treasures of three ancient and distinguished cavalry regiments, now brought together as The Royal Scots Dragoon Guards (Carabiniers & Greys).

The Regiment, Scotland's only regular cavalry regiment, is now 310 years old. Its three component parts were formed in the troubled years of the last quarter of the seventeenth century and, in the three centuries since then, have served their royal and political masters all over the globe, accumulating ninety battle honours in the process. As it stands today, the Regiment is part of the Royal Armoured Corps and its operational role is centred upon forming part of the ground-based shield for NATO on its eastern flank. Just as the nature of warfare, and of the training for warfare, is constantly changing, so the role of the Regiment has been modified, and it is now very different from the 'traditional' function of cavalry in the years before the machine-gun hamstrung the horse. But the nature of soldiering is that there will always be constants, always things which hardly change at all. Many of the objects which reflect both the changes and the constants will be found illustrating the pages of this book.

By way of background, it will be necessary to introduce the regimental components of the present Regiment. The 3rd and the 6th Dragoon Guards began life as regiments of Horse – cavalry pure and simple. As regiments of Horse, they preceded the 2nd Dragoons, far better known as the Royal Scots Greys, for the simple reason that Dragoons originally combined the mobility of the Horse with the fighting capabilities of the Foot and, as such, were placed in order of precedence after the regiments of Horse but before the regiments of Foot in the

Army List. The Greys, though, were the eldest of the three regiments which finally amalgamated in 1971, the 3rd and 6th Dragoon Guards having been amalgamated fifty years earlier. For much of their three-hundred-year history the three regiments served separately and had little in common. This history, the first attempt to tell the history of the present Regiment and all its predecessors in one slim volume, is therefore divided in each chapter into sections which reflect this separation.

Its innovative nature notwithstanding, this regimental history cannot hope to be comprehensive within the limit of one volume and, as I have explained, its *raison d'être* lies principally, if not exclusively, in illustrating the story of Scotland's cavalry regiment with the aid of its treasures. Far more comprehensive books dealing with aspects of the history of the Regiment exist, and these will be found in the Bibliography at the end of the book. It is to these far more worthy, if rather different, works that I direct the attention of those frustrated in their quest for knowledge by this one.

Stephen Wood
Edinburgh Castle
September 1988

CHAPTER ONE

Horse, Carabiniers and Dragoons

1678-1763

The Horse

The 4th Regiment of Horse was raised in June 1685 as six separate troops in the English counties of Worcestershire, Oxfordshire, Northamptonshire, Bedfordshire, Huntingdonshire and Middlesex. Each troop was commanded by a captain, who was assisted by a lieutenant and a cornet (or second lieutenant), and consisted of sixty troopers, each of whom had to provide his own horse, two trumpeters and three corporals; a troop quartermaster completed the muster roll.

The warrants commanding the raising of the separate Troops of Horse were dated 23 June, scarcely more than four months after the accession of the last Stuart King of Britain, James II of England and VII of Scotland. James combined a rather un-Stuart-like interest in his armed forces with a wholly Stuart-like disregard for either the consequences of his actions or the views of his advisors. Consequently, he was brazenly Catholic in an age when Catholicism was associated with despotism and in a country which was largely Protestant and moving inexorably towards theories of constitutional government. Earlier in June, his illegitimate nephew, James Scott, Duke of Monmouth, had landed in Dorset and begun a rebellion against his uncle. In historical retrospect, we can see that Monmouth's rebellion never really stood a chance, since it attracted little or no support from the cautious men of influence whose memories stretched back to the Civil Wars, but its advent led to the raising of many regiments which are with us still. Troops which eventually became the 4th Horse were not engaged at the Battle of

Thomas Windsor, 7th Baron Windsor and 1st Earl of Plymouth (1627?-1687), 1st Colonel of the 3rd Dragoon Guards (1685-1687). Artist unknown

Sedgmoor, which ended the Rebellion; the termination of that unequal and brief struggle was left to more seasoned soldiers. The King, however, had had a small fright and had not yet so far alienated his Parliament that they were prepared to oppose his wishes when he asked for a vote of money to keep some of his new Army in being. Consequently, on 15 July 1685, the same day that the Duke of Monmouth lost his head to the axe of Jack Ketch the executioner, James was able to sign a warrant appointing Thomas, 1st Earl of Plymouth, to the colonelcy of the 4th Regiment of Horse.

Although the Regiment was ranked as 4th among the Regiments of Horse for the next sixty years, it was more frequently known by the name of the Colonel. When the Colonel changed, and the Regiment changed Colonels eight times before the practice finally ceased in 1751, the Regiment's name changed. When the six troops were regimented, the number of troopers was reduced to forty per troop and a major, an adjutant, a chaplain, a surgeon and a kettledrummer were taken on to the regimental strength. The kettledrummer was paid three shillings a day, twice the pay of a trooper but the same as that of a corporal, or about fifteen to twenty pounds in today's currency. From this apparent largesse would be deducted, though, the cost of feeding himself and his horse, stabling for the latter and the cost of replacing the standard items of his uniform.

King James used his Army for increasingly political motives, principally to bolster his position as an embryonic absolute monarch. Recalcitrant towns and cities, refusing to accept the King's pro-Catholic measures, found that they had regiments forcibly billeted upon them. Not only had they to feed and house the soldiers, and their horses in the case of cavalry, but the towns found, in many cases, that the soldiers had been created freemen of the borough, an action that allowed the unwelcome guests actively to participate in elections. In Huntingdon in 1688 soldiers of the 4th Horse were thus used as political pawns in the chess-game that the King was playing with decreasing subtlety.

The Revolution of 1688 tested the loyalty of much of the Army, although several senior officers – including John Churchill, later Duke of Marlborough – had been negotiating with Prince William of Orange for some time before he arrived at Torbay in November 1688. Once William landed, the trickle of desertions towards him swelled into a stream – principally of commissioned ranks – and the impression remains that this gradual winnowing of leadership from James's Army only exacerbated the general despondency within it. James's flight to France left his Army bereft of the sovereign to whom loyalty had been sworn, and it was thus a relatively straightforward task for William to adopt the Army's allegiance, once it had been purged of Catholics.

While the transfer of the monarchy from James to William and Mary had been relatively peacefully achieved in England, it led to a minor rebellion in Scotland and a major campaign in Ireland. Although the 4th Horse were spared participation in the latest of the Irish troubles, they were involved in what came to be regarded as the first Jacobite rebellion in Scotland. Led by James Graham, Viscount Dundee, a small and far from homogeneous force of Highlanders and other disaffected Episcopalian and Catholic Scots led a government Army, including the 4th Horse, a merry dance throughout the Highlands. The Regiment, unused to campaigning at all and especially not in the inhospitable climate of Highland Scotland, gradually depleted its resources and was recuperating in Lowland Scotland when Dundee's Highlanders cut up the government forces at Killiecrankie in July 1689. They did, however, form part of the reinforcements which, aided by the death of Dundee at Killiecrankie, rolled up the rebellion relatively quickly.

The accession of William III and his consort Mary, apart from securing the Protestant succession and the gradual development of constitutional government, brought Britain straight into the front line of a long series of wars with France. For William, the acquisition of Britain meant that he was at last able to turn the flank of Louis XIV, King of France, and use British soldiers alongside his Dutch to help him resist the most powerful land force in Europe. In 1691, therefore, the 4th Horse were transferred to Flanders in preparation for William's spring offensive of 1692 against Louis XIV. The Regiment remained quartered in the Low Countries until the Peace of Ryswick in 1697 provided a kind of truce with France. In the intervening five years they had been involved in sieges, and in relieving sieges, in small-scale skirmishes and thundering, knee-to-knee cavalry actions as at Neerlanden in July 1693. Throughout the whole campaign Flanders had lived up to its reputation as a poor and dispiriting place in which to conduct a war; the land was poor, the climate depressing, supplies infrequent and pay intermittent. The return to Britain in 1697 must have seemed like a welcome release, despite the inevitable reduction in the size of the Regiment that was ordered by Parliament immediately upon the cessation of active hostilities.

From its wartime strength of just less than three hundred officers and men, the Regiment reduced to a peacetime establishment of two hundred and thirty. For the next five years, though, its duties were domestic and ceremonial, centred on the Court – which moved as the King moved, until William's death in 1702.

In 1701 James II and VI had breathed his last in exile at St Germain-en-Laye and his son had been immediately recognised by Louis XIV as rightful King. Such recognition was in direct contravention of the Treaty of Ryswick and, added to Louis's machinations concerning the succession to the Spanish throne of his grandson, provided ample cause for the resumption of the war. The 4th Horse disembarked for Flanders again in March 1702. After two years of meandering rather aimlessly around the mud of Flanders, the 4th Horse was incorporated in Marlborough's march to the Danube, a trek of two hundred and fifty miles in six weeks which culminated in the successful battles of the Schellenberg and Blenheim in July and August 1704. No accurate returns appear to have been kept of other ranks of the 4th Horse who were killed or wounded in these two actions, the second of which subsequently became the Regiment's first battle honour, but it is recorded that two officers and forty-seven horses perished at Blenheim, with five officers sustaining wounds.

After another two years of feinting at the French lines, of skirmishes and of marching and counter-marching, the 4th Horse were engaged at the Battle of Ramillies in May 1706 against a combined army of French, Spanish and Bavarian soldiers. As well as obtaining another battle honour, the Regiment is also recorded as having captured the standard and kettledrums of the Elector of Bavaria's Guard; unfortunately no record of their fate exists today. A further successful engagement at Oudenarde in July 1708 was fought, this time with the 4th Horse re-equipped with steel, supposedly pistol-proof, breastplates. The Regiment's use of armour had been intermittent since its foundation and breastplates had not been brought when they embarked in 1702. Despite the protection provided by the steel cuirasses, they were uncomfortable and were recorded as interfering with the free movement of the sword arm. A fourth battle honour followed for participation at the Pyrrhic victory of Malplaquet in September 1709 and, for the following four years, the Regiment was engaged, with the rest of the Army, in laying successful sieges to a series of towns on the French border. After the end of the war, in 1713, the Regiment returned home and was again reduced in size.

A trooper of the Royal Regiment of North British Dragoons, 1742. From A Representation of the CLOATHING of His Majesty's Houshold, and of all the Forces upon the Establishments of GREAT BRITAIN AND IRELAND, *1742.*

A trooper in the uniform of both the 4th Regiment of Horse and 1st Regiment of Carabiniers, 1742 The illustration, taken from A Representation of the CLOATHING of His Majesty's Houshold, and of all the Forces upon the Establishments of GREAT BRITAIN AND IRELAND, *1742, indicates that the styles of the uniforms were similar, only the facing colours differentiating between the two regiments: the 4th Horse having white facing, the Carabiniers yellow.*

The death of Queen Anne in 1714 was followed by the accession of George, Elector of Hanover, and by the outbreak of another Jacobite rebellion in Scotland. Western England, especially Lancashire, seems to have been the traditional power-base of Jacobitism south of the border, but a nest of Jacobites was reported to exist in Bath in 1715 and the 4th Horse were ordered to investigate. A number of citizens were persuaded to help the soldiers with their enquiries and several caches of weapons were discovered and impounded. The Jacobite *débâcle* of 1715 had not killed the movement, however, and the next three or four decades were to be characterised by frequent Jacobite scares. Although occasionally justified, these chiefly resulted in Scotland and things Scottish being deeply distrusted by government supporters in England (who blithely ignored the fact that few Scots actually had active Jacobite sympathies). The Colonel of the 4th Horse from 1717 to 1748 was General, later Field Marshal, George Wade who, as

Commander-in-Chief in Scotland from 1725 to 1740, did his bit, by encouraging fort- and road-building, to bring the Highlands within reach of the Redcoats' bayonets. The Regiment was involved on the fringes of the Jacobite Rebellion of 1745-46, and in action (briefly) at Clifton near Penrith in December 1745.

George II, who had succeeded his father as King in 1727, was a monarch whose interest in his Army amounted almost to interference, but whose memory later generations of military costume historians have had cause to bless since the paintings and engravings that the King and his son the Duke of Cumberland commissioned in the 1740s and 1750s remain the only reliable record of how British soldiers were dressed and equipped at that time.

In a period of comparative freedom from foreign entanglements, George II was, however, forced to heed the economic arguments of his advisors and agree to changes in the Army. In 1747, therefore, the Regiment so long ranked as the 4th Horse was regraded as the 3rd Dragoon Guards; a regrading that was effectively a demotion both in status and in pay, but one which was softened by the use of "Guards" in the title. To all intents and purposes, the Regiment had become Dragoons: medium cavalry, armed and largely dressed as infantry, yet expected to fight as both. Appreciating the implicit slap in the face that he had dealt for reasons of economic expediency, the King ordered that the three newly-created regiments of Dragoon Guards would take precedence over all other regiments of Dragoons in his Army.

Domestic duties continued for the Regiment prior to the outbreak of the Seven Years War in 1756 and manifested themselves in tours of duty both inland and on the coast of England at a time when no police or customs force existed and a perceived threat of further Jacobite rebellions refused to vanish. In 1755, war being imminent, the Regiment was brought up to strength by the addition of 100 men, and shortly afterwards a light troop was added to the existing six troops. This latter troop was the result of the observation of the success of light cavalry, in the skirmishing, reconnaissance and other roles demanding swift and unencumbered movement, during the War of the Austrian Succession (1740-48). In 1758 it was brigaded with eight other similar troops from other Dragoon and Dragoon Guards regiments for offensive action against the French coast. Although not wholly successful, the establishment of the light troops of Dragoons – which were disbanded at the end of the war in 1763 – led rapidly to the raising of specific regiments of Light Dragoons.

The Regiment as a whole arrived in Germany in 1758 but saw little action until the battles of Corpach and Warburg in 1760, achieving considerable losses at the former engagement and minimal ones, and a battle honour, at the latter. The winter of 1760 was passed in quarters in Paderborn, an area not unknown to

British regiments in more recent years, and for the following two years of the war the 3rd Dragoon Guards were occupied in relatively small-scale actions and skirmishes.

The Carabiniers

The 9th Regiment of Horse dates its existence from June 1685, and for the same reason as that of the 4th Horse: Monmouth's rebellion. The six troops, originally independent but regimented after the end of the rebellion, were rather more scattered in origin than those of the 4th Horse, coming from Hampshire, Nottinghamshire, Hertfordshire, Yorkshire – in Doncaster, Suffolk and, probably, Devon. The 9th Horse was regimented on 30 July 1685 and, like the other regiments of Horse, each man was armed and equipped with a cuirass, a steel helmet – probably with ear, neck and nose protection, a pair of pistols, a sword and a carbine. The carbine, which was shortly to become so much associated with the Regiment, was a short musket of slightly smaller bore than that of the infantryman's musket. Carbines had been issued to regiments of Horse since the early 1670s and were not, in 1685 or later, unique to the 9th Horse.

Like the 4th Horse, the 9th underwent frequent changes of title as its Colonels changed between 1685 and 1751 (seventeen Colonels in sixty-six years in the case of the 9th) but these changes were complicated still further by the array of other names by which the Regiment was also known. Its first Colonel, Lord Lumley, had been Master of the Horse and Treasurer to Charles II's Queen, Catherine of Braganza, after Charles's death known as the Queen Dowager. Because of this association the Regiment was accorded the title "The Queen Dowager's Regiment of Horse" until 1692, despite the fact that Lumley relinquished the colonelcy after eighteen months.

Lumley's independent troop was engaged in the mopping-up operations after the battle of Sedgmoor in 1685 and was responsible for Monmouth's capture and transportation to London. The colonelcy of the 9th was Lumley's reward, but it seems that he found the atmosphere of James's court uncomfortable and eventually resigned in consequence. It may be, of course, that he was already corresponding with Prince William of Orange, who created him 1st Earl of Scarbrough shortly after becoming King.

The Regiment's first active service was seen during the campaign in Ireland between 1689 and 1691. Dundee's rebellion in Scotland was little more than a side-show by comparison with the reaction that James's expulsion from the British throne provoked in Ireland. The island was, of course, ideally situated for

Richard Lumley, 1st Baron and 1st Viscount Lumley, 1st Earl of Scarbrough (d.1721). 1st Colonel of the 6th Dragoon Guards (1685-1687). Artist unknown.

insurrection against mainland Britain and, to the great delight of France and frustration of William, tied up considerable British forces throughout the two-year struggle. After several uncomfortable months in Ireland, foraging for supplies from the land and suffering numerous casualties from the effects of the climate, the Regiment eventually formed part of William's forces which faced those of James at the Battle of the Boyne in July 1690. After the battle came an attempt to take Limerick by storm, and after that several months of anti-guerrilla warfare against those supporters of James who had taken to the hills to continue his cause in unorthodox ways. Throughout the campaign the Regiment was constantly noticed by King William and, as a result of a distinguished part in an unfortunate campaign, was dignified by him with the additional title of "Carabiniers" in 1692. Two years earlier it had been advanced up the order of precedence of Regiments of Horse to eighth position, but the honorific title of "Carabiniers" stuck and, indeed, is with us still. Its use seems to have come and gone during the first sixty or so years of the Regiment possessing the additional title. Some documents employ it, some ignore it, but – for the period covered by this chapter – despite its intermittence, it will avoid confusion if the Regiment is referred to as the Carabiniers.

In April 1692 the Regiment landed in the Low Countries as part of the force of fifty thousand British soldiers with which William embarked in order to pursue his war against France. Apart from a small amount of involvement at the battle of

Lieutenant-Colonel Philip Chenevix, who commanded the Carabiniers from 1745 to 1750. Chenevix's father, also Philip, was the son of a refugee French Huguenot pastor and, as the Regiment's major, was killed in action at the Battle of Blenheim in 1704. Artist unknown

Steinkirk in August, the Carabiniers saw little action in their first year in Flanders but were with the 4th Horse at the battle of Neerlanden in July 1693. One of the officers of the Carabiniers, Cornelius Wood, had so persistently distinguished himself, in Ireland as well as in Flanders, that he was rewarded in December 1693 by the colonelcy of the 4th Horse; the first of many links that were to bind the two regiments together. The two regiments fought alongside each other for much of the campaign and, indeed, constituted the only cavalry in William's Army in Brabant during 1696. At the Peace of Ryswick the Carabiniers returned home to an instant reduction in size, considerable arrears of pay and five years of domestic postings and duties.

The Regiment returned to Brabant in March 1702 and, like the 4th Horse, spent some time defending the Low Countries against French aggression before participating in Marlborough's march to Ulm on the Danube. The Carabiniers were with both the 4th Horse and the Greys at the assault on the Schellenberg and were in the thick of the fighting at Blenheim, at which battle they lost five officers and eighty-six horses. Amongst the dead was the Major, Philip Chenevix, the son of a French Huguenot refugee. His widow and three children received a bounty of one hundred and sixty-two pounds after his death and one of his sons, also Philip, served in the Regiment from 1711 until 1750, commanding it as Lieutenant-Colonel for the last five years of his service.

In 1705 and 1706 the Carabiniers added to the number of their battle trophies, capturing the standard of the Bavarian Horse Guards in an affray in Flanders in 1705 and that of the French Royal Regiment of Bombardiers, together with several pieces of ordnance, at the Battle of Ramillies the following year. In line with the usual practice of the time, it is probable that these captured standards were sent to the Royal Hospital in Chelsea where the passage of the years, and atmospheric pollution, has destroyed them. Much of the remainder of the campaign, until the end of the war, was passed in the same theatre of war as that of the 4th Horse; the Carabiniers too getting back their cuirasses in 1707. The Regiment fought at Oudenarde and at Malplaquet, as did the 4th Horse, and were surprised and nearly overrun during a night attack by the French on their camp at Arleux, but recovered to be present at the capture of Bouchain, which effectively ended the war.

At the Treaty of Utrecht in 1713 the Regiment returned to garrison duties in Ireland, being placed in momentary states of readiness during the 1715 and 1719 Jacobite rebellions but seeing no action.

Other than the War of the Austrian Succession, which included such famous battles as Dettingen and Fontenoy, the period between 1713 and 1756 was marked as one of relative peace as far as the majority of the British Army was concerned. The Carabiniers remained unaffected by the 1745 Jacobite rebellion and remained stationed in Ireland until 1760, a total of forty-seven years. Such records as exist of the Regiment's history deal fleetingly with this period, and so one must assume that Ireland was relatively quiet, even during the 1745 rebellion. The Regiment provided sixty or so men and horses in 1743 and 1744 to augment the Army on the continent of Europe that had suffered losses during the War of the Austrian Succession.

As a result of the changes in designation of the Regiments of Horse to those of Dragoon Guards in 1747, the Carabiniers were advanced up the order of precedence to take their place in the *Army List* as the "3rd Regiment of (Irish) Horse or Carabiniers". The "Irish" part of the title seems to have been little used and had certainly been dropped by 1756.

The Carabiniers arrived in Germany in 1760, bringing the British Army's cavalry strength up to thirteen regiments and, although they missed actual action at the battle of Corpach, were heavily involved at Warburg in July. The Carabiniers wintered in Paderborn too in 1760 and spent much of the following year campaigning in that part of Germany, manoeuvring and skirmishing with the French Army. Few actions of any consequence were fought, and the majority of British casualties were caused by disease or desertion. The war dragged to a close in 1762 and the Carabiniers left Germany for Ireland in the following year, being reduced to a peacetime establishment of barely one hundred and fifty men.

The Dragoons

Late seventeenth century Scotland was a troubled place; more so, it may be said, than her neighbour to the south. The Restoration of the monarchy in 1660 had been followed by attempts, of gradually increasing severity, to impose upon Scotland a form of church government not markedly dissimilar to that operated by the Church of England: Episcopacy. The protagonists of Presbyterianism in Scotland saw this as yet another attempt to subvert them and their country to increasing control from London, and resisted it accordingly. It seems incomprehensible now, in the late twentieth century, that issues of religion could have been of such importance, even in Scotland, but the growth of civil disobedience was such in some parts of the country, especially in the south-west, that government saw no alternative to a policy of active repression of Presbyterianism. Religious disobedience was equated with nascent treason and treated accordingly.

Another factor of the period, which again seems unthinkable now, was the normality of the use of military forces to suppress civilian disturbances. Such use of soldiers would continue until well after the establishment of permanent police forces in the mid nineteenth century, and the ideal soldier-policeman for European governments of the seventeenth century was the Dragoon. Louis XIV, King of France, had employed the *Dragonnade* (brutal measures to enforce his religious laws) after the revocation of the Edict of Nantes in 1685 removed the right to freedom of worship from his Protestant subjects, and the measures taken by his secret friend, Charles II, in the Scotland of the 1660s and 1670s closely resembled the harrying repressive policies of the French King. Armed, organised and equipped like infantrymen, dragoons were mounted and so much faster across country, especially rocky or boggy country, than ordinary foot-soldiers. Dragoons were also cheaper than Horse since their rate of pay was lower.

The derivation of their title has been a matter for controversy, but it seems likely that it is associated with the name of a type of heavy carbine of the early seventeenth century, which was known as a "dragon". It is also, of course, quite possible that the dragon took its name from its users; but that must remain a puzzle for etymologists. Whatever the case, seventeenth century dragoons were also frequently armed with muskets, genuine carbines or musketoons – this latter firearm being so similar to a dragon that they were probably the same thing at the time. Whereas the dragon, or musketoon, seems frequently to have had a bore similar to that of an infantryman's musket (about 12 bore in the 1620s), the true carbine was actually a short musket with a much smaller bore (about 24 bore in the 1630s).

A model of a trooper, Royal Regiment of North British Dragoons, c. 1745. This model, made of leather, metal, papier-mâché and other mixed media, is probably a contemporary item, perhaps made for a child. Its attention both to detail and to accuracy is remarkable and strengthens the belief in its age.

Presbyterianism seemed to be thriving on ineffectual attempts to persecute it by the 1670s, and its adherents regularly attended conventicles – open-air prayer meetings with sentries posted to warn of approaching soldiers. Attempts to stamp out religious dissent appeared to be in need of assistance, and so three companies of Dragoons were raised in Scotland in 1678. Dragoons, being essentially infantry with horses, were arranged by company and not yet by troop and, unlike regiments of Horse, had sergeants as well as corporals. The increase in the government forces had quite the opposite effect of driving the Presbyterians underground, and the authorities in Scotland rapidly found themselves faced with a full-scale rebellion. Actions at Drumclog and Bothwell Bridge resulted in 1679; the latter battle overcompensating in its success for the defeat of a small government force at the former. The three Scottish companies of Dragoons were involved at Bothwell Bridge, where the government forces were commanded by the Duke of Monmouth, and also in the following year at Airds Moss. In 1681, so successful had the counter-insurgency campaign been, a further three companies of Dragoons were raised and the six companies formed into a Regiment of Dragoons under the colonelcy of Lieutenant-General Thomas Dalzell.

Dalzell was a remarkable man by any standards. A soldier all his adult life, he first saw action in the La Rochelle expedition of 1628. In the 1640s he was in Ireland, earning himself a reputation for exemplary ferocity, against his own deserters as much as against the Irish. Captured whilst fighting for Charles II at the Battle of Worcester in 1650, he was imprisoned in the Tower, but escaped to join his King in France and then returned to Scotland to oppose the

Lieutenant-General Thomas Dalzell of the Binns (1599?-1685). 1st Colonel of the Royal Scots Greys (1681-1685). Artist: L Schunemann

Parliamentarian forces in the campaign of 1654. Returning to France briefly, he then travelled to Russia and fought for the Tsar for ten years until, as a Russian general, he was summoned home by the restored King Charles. He was Commander-in-Chief in Scotland in 1666 and 1667 and again from 1679 until his death in 1685. An uncompromising disciplinarian with a hatred of Covenanting Presbyterians amounting almost to mania, he drafted the Articles of War for the Forces in Scotland in 1667; of the eighty-six Articles, forty-two specified the death penalty for offences and several others offered a sentence of mutilation.

Dalzell's Dragoons were involved in the suppression of the Earl of Argyll's rebellion in 1685, an event which followed the death of Charles II and accession of James II and VII and was a Scottish equivalent of Monmouth's rebellion in the west of England. They were called south by James as part of the Scottish forces, on whose loyalty he hoped he could still rely, in 1688, when invasion by Prince William of Orange appeared imminent. At the Revolution of 1688 the Regiment's loyalties were severely tested and clearly divided and, while the Colonel changed – as was normal throughout the Army – several officers remained loyal to the old régime once the Regiment returned to Scotland in 1689. Although the Regiment avoided involvement in the Battle of Killiecrankie in 1689, they were part of the force which pursued the Jacobites both before and after that action and actively participated in the final rout of the Jacobites at Cromdale on Speyside in 1690.

The Regiment's title as "The Royal Regiment of Scots Dragoons" was confirmed in 1692, and by 1693 the Regiment was mounted on the grey horses which would eventually provide its subtitle. In common with most of the rest of the British Army, the Dragoons embarked for the Low Countries in 1694 and campaigned there, without much action, until the Peace of Ryswick in 1697. On return to Britain the regimental strength was almost halved and two entire companies disbanded. Captain Andrew Agnew, younger of Lochryan, who had bought a grey horse in 1693, received instructions to downgrade his youngest sergeant and corporal, to pay his quartermaster as a sergeant and to tell his adjutant to do the quartermaster's job. Financial stringencies affecting the peacetime Army are one of the many things which never change; neither are put-upon adjutants.

On the resumption of the war in 1702 the Regiment was brought up to strength and left Britain for Brabant, where it spent two years with the rest of the forces on some fairly desultory campaigning and besieging of frontier towns before joining Marlborough's march to the Danube. The Regiment fought as infantry at the Battle of the Schellenberg at Donauwerth, losing eight killed and eighteen wounded. At Blenheim they lost no one, but contributed to the victory by driving the fleeing French back into the village of Blenheim, where they had little choice but to surrender. The Regimental prize money for the Schellenberg and Blenheim was apportioned according to rank in the manner standard at the period: the Colonel received £150, whilst each of the troopers gained £1.50 (multiply by 100 for 1988 values).

Participation at the Battle of Ramillies followed in 1706, at the end of which the Regiment captured the colours of the French *Régiment du Roi.* Among the more serious casualties of the battle was Christian Welsh, a dragoon who had served as a Grey for four years without her gender being either obvious or discovered. Her husband has, as husbands will, gone for a soldier some time before, and for reasons not recorded she had followed him. The errant husband was eventually reconciled with his wife but was killed shortly afterwards. Taken up by a Captain Ross, who was also killed, she eventually married a soldier called Davies, and both became in-pensioners of the Royal Hospital, Chelsea. Christian Davies died in 1739 and was buried in Chelsea.

The Act of Union of 1707, which united the Parliaments of England and Scotland and further reduced the independence of Scotland, resulted in the Regiment becoming titled as the "Royal Regiment of North British Dragoons". The Greys fought at Oudenarde in 1708 and at Malplaquet in 1709, where they sustained about thirty casualties following severe fighting. The remainder of the War of the Spanish Succession saw the Regiment fully engaged in the capture of

A trooper's cap, Royal Regiment of North British Dragoons, c. 1742. Probably captured or lost during the War of the Austrian Succession and now preserved in the Musée de l'Armée, Paris.

An officer, thought to be Captain-Lieutenant Andrew Agnew, Royal Regiment of North British Dragoons, c. 1713. Andrew Agnew (1687-1771), later Lieutenant-General Sir Andrew Agnew of Lochnaw, Bart., transferred to the Royal North British Fuzileers (later the Royal Scots Fusiliers) in 1718 and commanded that regiment at the Battle of Dettingen 1743. Artist unknown

the line of French frontier forts and it seems, from all accounts of their part in the War, that they were increasingly becoming engaged as cavalry and not as true Dragoons.

Returning home in 1713, the Regiment was actually increased in strength to nine companies, although these companies seem gradually to have been called troops more frequently in the existing records. This augmentation was only temporary though, since in 1715, upon the threat of another Jacobite rebellion following the accession of King George I, three troops were sliced off to be incorporated in the newly re-raised 7th Dragoons, and so the Greys were reduced to six troops. The Regiment moved to Scotland and camped at Stirling to await developments and, in October, skirmished with a party of Jacobite soldiers in Dunfermline. An atmosphere of panic seems to have infected Britain during the 1715 rebellion, and rumours and counter-rumours were allowed to pass for

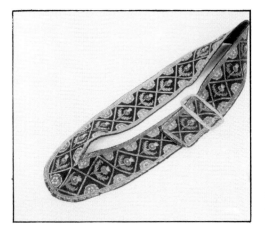

Guidon belt, Royal Regiment of North British Dragoons, c. 1754. Associated with Lieutenant-General David Home, who served with the Regiment from 1754 until 1802, commanding it from 1779 to 1794.

factual information. The Greys spent some weeks in the Lowlands, marching through Kinross, capturing a ship off Burntisland and breaking a few heads in Leith while the large forces of both sides attempted to come to grips with each other. In November, on the rolling moor outside Dunblane known as Sheriffmuir, the two armies met; the Greys on the right flank of the government forces defeating and chasing the Jacobite cavalry for some miles.

For the next five years, until the signing of peace in 1720, the Regiment formed a kind of mobile garrison in Scotland intended to thwart any further attempts at Jacobite-inspired, and Spanish-funded, insurrections. Three troops of the Regiment were involved at the Battle of Glenshiel in 1719 against a few shivering Spaniards and the usual ragged crew of opportunist Highlanders. During the next two decades the Greys were stationed throughout Britain, and varied in establishment from six to nine troops, depending upon the likelihood of foreign adventures. Their duties were principally those of mounted policemen or in giving assistance to customs officers against smugglers.

In 1742 the Regiment embarked for the War of the Austrian Succession and participated in the battles of Dettingen in 1743, at which they captured a standard of the French Household Cavalry, and Fontenoy in 1745, at which indecisive battle the Colonel, Lieutenant-General Sir James Campbell, lost a leg and subsequently died. Lost, too, at one of these battles, was at least one of the new tall "mitre" caps which the Regiment had worn for only a few years: it is now one of the trophies kept in the Musée de l'Armée in Paris. The Regiment was ordered home in 1745 to help resist the Jacobite rebellion, but encountered bad weather, which delayed the troopships, and by the time that the weather allowed sailing the

Lieutenant-Colonel John Forbes, who commanded the Royal Regiment of North British Dragoons 1750-57. John Forbes (1710-1759), was commissioned into the Regiment in 1735 and left it to become a Brigadier during the Seven Years War in America. Commanding an expedition to the French-held Fort Duquesne, he died shortly afterwards, but not before naming the captured fort Pitts-Bourgh. Artist: T Robertson Aikman (dates unknown)

rebellion was over. At the battle of Laffeldt in 1747 a charge by the Greys, the Inniskilling (6th) and the Queens Own (7th) Dragoons saved defeat from becoming a rout, although at a cost to the Greys of casualties comprising over one-third of their strength.

The Regiment returned home in 1748 and was stationed throughout England for the next decade. In common with some other cavalry regiments, the Greys had a light troop added in 1756 (which wore a distinctively different head-dress to the rest of the Regiment), and this troop was one of those which formed what might now be called a "commando", for raids on the French coast after the outbreak of the Seven Years War in 1756.

The Lieutenant-Colonel in command of the Regiment from 1750 was John Forbes, who left the Greys in 1757 to be appointed a Brigadier-General in America. He led a successful expedition against Fort Duquesne in 1758 and, despite being so ill throughout that he had to be carried in a litter, directed the assault which persuaded the French to surrender the fort. In reporting the success of his mission to his superiors, Forbes made the first recorded use of the name "Pitts-Bourgh" to describe the renamed fortification and, subsequently, the city of Pittsburgh grew around the fort.

The Regiment as a whole left for Germany in 1758 and were in action at the battles of Minden in 1759 and of Warburg in 1760, suffering minimal casualties. The remainder of the campaign was relatively uneventful, and the Greys returned to Britain in 1763, moving north to Scotland at the end of that year.

CHAPTER TWO

Securing An Empire

1764-1815

3rd Dragoon Guards

The Regiment returned home, to quarters in Canterbury, early in 1763 to have its establishment reduced and its light troop disbanded. The potential of light cavalry had not gone unnoticed, though, even if its use had been a little unco-ordinated, and so each cavalry regiment, or at least those who had contributed their light troop to the Brigade, was instructed to arm and equip eight men per troop as light cavalrymen. In real terms, all this meant was that they were trained in reconnaissance and skirmishing and reduced in armament to just a sword and pair of pistols (which they had to be able to load and fire while moving); their uniforms and mounts remained unchanged.

In 1765 the Regiment was granted the subsidiary title (or The Prince of Wales's), the other two regiments of Dragoon Guards being The King's (1st) and The Queen's (2nd), and all its appointments were altered to incorporate the badges and devices associated with HRH The Prince of Wales, who was just three years old at the time but who eventually became King George IV. The practice of giving honorary titles of this kind to regiments grew inexorably through the eighteenth and nineteenth centuries and was aided by the large families of King George III and Queen Victoria, the majority of whose offspring managed, at some point, to have their title (or that of their consort or children) associated with one or more British regiments. The use of the personal title in a regiment's title did not always indicate personal associations with the regiment concerned.

In the years between the ending of the Seven Years War (1763) and the beginning of the wars against Revolutionary France (1793) the Regiment remained in Britain, being quartered in a wide variety of locations from Scotland to the south coast. The docking of the horses' tails was stopped in 1764 and trumpeters replaced drummers on the regimental establishment in 1766. Despite Britain being at peace, it was really a period of cold war with the French who, it was felt by the British Government, would seize every opportunity to make a nuisance of themselves. The threat of Jacobitism was ever present, and was regarded almost as a potential fifth column, even though its figurehead was fast becoming a pathetic drink-sodden figure who actually presented little real danger to Britain's stability. Smuggling continued, and the Regiment maintained its position as mounted policemen in aid of the customs and excise authorities. The outbreak of war with the thirteen colonies of the embryonic United States of America in 1775 resulted in a slight increase in the establishments of most regiments, but the Regiment remained uninvolved. The American Revolutionary War was principally fought by infantry and light cavalry, the country and tactics of the enemy being far from suited for the traditional shock-tactic role of heavy cavalry.

A combination of the danger from France and that presented by Jacobitism – both seen as being linked with the supposed mendacity of the Roman Catholic Church – meant that it was never difficult throughout the eighteenth century to whip up anti-Catholic hysteria, especially among the London mob, whose reputation and capacity for rapacious violence was, justifiably, internationally notorious. When the government, aware that the Catholic and Jacobite threat was far more imaginary than real by the late 1770s, attempted to relax the anti-Catholic laws in order to be able to recruit Catholics into the Army for the war in America, a war that had suddenly been made serious by the intervention of France on the side of the revolutionary colonists, widespread rioting resulted. This became particularly serious in London in 1780 and, because of their orchestration by Lord George Gordon – a less than entirely sane M.P. and vehement Protestant – the riots are known to historians as the Gordon riots. By the time that the Regiment arrived from Shrewsbury to back up the troops already engaged against the rioters, large parts of London were no-go areas for the authorities and a great deal of damage had been done to the property of real and suspected Catholics or pro-Catholics. The Regiment was involved in suppressing the riots, but no detailed records exist of their actual part in restoring law and order.

A further decade of postings within Britain followed until 1793, when four troops of the Regiment embarked for the war in the Low Countries that had begun against the Army of Revolutionary France. The force of which they were part was commanded by the younger brother of the Prince of Wales, Prince Frederick, Duke of York, a career soldier whose exploits in Flanders were to be celebrated in a children's nursery rhyme. At this period little attention was given to training for war, and operations against smugglers or a discontented civilian population had done little to prepare the Regiment, after thirty years of peacetime service, for the realities of what they were to encounter on the continent. Initially successful, the campaign literally floundered when the French redoubled their attacks on British positions that had become waterlogged by the opening of the dykes. Having fought their way out of the resulting morass the British went on to conduct a campaign in alliance with the Austrians, Dutch, and Prussians, an alliance that rapidly collapsed in the face of mounting French strength and success in battle. The Regiment took a major part in two actions at Beaumont and at Willems, both of which demonstrated how far their training had improved through battlefield experience, and both of which showed British cavalry in their most effective light. At Willems the Regiment was part of a cavalry attack that managed to break into a number of French squares of infantry, a rare occurrence even for French infantry. The winter of 1794 was an appallingly harsh one and Britain's allies were making their excuses and leaving so, in 1795, the British force re-embarked for England, leaving northern continental Europe to the largely uninterrupted rule of France for the next two decades.

With France triumphant on the continent, and Britain bereft of allies, virtually all troops in Britain were placed on an anti-invasion footing until after the naval Battle of Trafalgar in 1805. In this, they were accompanied by hastily-raised units of volunteer infantry and yeomanry cavalry, whose enthusiasm and pride in their dashing appearance made them objects of cynical amusement for the regular troops who had experienced the reality of conflict. The Regiment was quartered in England until 1803, when it moved to Scotland for a year prior to embarkation for Ireland, where it remained until 1808. Together with fears of invasion, from France, government was all too aware – to an occasionally exaggerated extent – that some of its subjects might not be averse to the replacement of the British monarchy by a government run on French revolutionary lines. Although this fear diminished slightly after the installation of Napoleon as Emperor in 1804, fear of foreign agents and a fifth column continued, especially in Ireland, and so the years prior to the beginning of the Peninsular War were far from relaxing ones for the 3rd Dragoon Guards.

Although the success of the Royal Navy had secured Britain against invasion, the government realised that France could not be defeated on land by the Navy and that, if the war was to be ended, a land defeat for France by the Army was essential. Invasion of the European continent was the only way that this could be achieved and, for a number of reasons, the Iberian peninsula offered the best site for a second front. Although an initial attempt in 1808 had failed, invasion was tried again in the following year and, in April 1809, the Regiment landed in Lisbon as part of a cavalry Brigade in the Army commanded by the then relatively

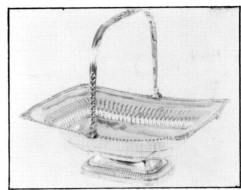

Silver cake basket from the Officers' Mess silver, 3rd Dragoon Guards, c. 1798. Hallmarks indistinct, maker possibly William Hall

unknown Lieutenant-General Sir Arthur Wellesley.

In the briefest terms, Wellesley's plans were centred upon an invasion of France via Spain, and he was aided in his goal by the fact that Napoleon had alienated the Spanish by imposing his brother upon them as King. Wellesley therefore had the support of both the Portuguese and Spanish armies, which were immense on paper – if less than wholly reliable in practice – together with the doubtful, if effective, help of Spanish partisans whose concept of warfare – especially against the French – was far from chivalrous. In order to get to France, starting from Portugal, the British and their allies had, therefore, to march across Spain. The journey took three years (1811-14) and every step of the way was bloodily contested by a series of French armies, commanded by a succession of French marshals. As his success rate mounted, so Sir Arthur Wellesley was promoted through each step of the peerage until, as Duke of Wellington, he entered France in 1814.

The 3rd Dragoon Guards' first major action was at Talavera in July 1809 which, like so many Peninsular battles, was principally an infantry engagement. The 3rd attempted to repeat their square-breaking success of Willems, but failed, and were principally used to contain the French and engage them on their flanks. Talavera was a bloody battle, resulting in some five thousand British casualties, and an indecisive one after which Wellington retreated into Portugal to regroup and to establish impregnable fortifications behind which his Army could recover and be reinforced. The 3rd, along with the other cavalry, covered the retreat, and frequently skirmished with the French advance guard in consequence. Effectively, the British remained under siege until 1811 when the French, disease-ridden and poorly supported, were forced to withdraw. Wellington broke out and, with the Regiment acting as scouts ahead of the part of the Army commanded by Major General William Beresford, moved into Spain again. At the battle of Albuhera in May 1811 the Regiment was placed on the right flank, and sustained small losses in decimating a French Lancer regiment in what was, again, a foot-soldiers' battle of appalling carnage.

The Peninsular War was characterised by sieges of strategically-sited cities, and the Regiment was present at those of Cuidad Rodrigo and Badajoz in 1812 as well as being used by Wellington in various manoeuvres intended to disguise his true intentions from the French. After a short retreat upon Cuidad Rodrigo in 1812, Wellington again advanced towards France in 1813, the rapidity of his progress taking the French rather by surprise. The 3rd Dragoon Guards were involved in the final rolling-up stages of the Battle of Vittoria in July 1813 and captured guns and supply wagons as well as routing a French column, in exchange for which action their casualties were minimal. The invasion of south-west France began in 1814, and, co-ordinated (largely by coincidence) with Napoleon's defeats in the east, ended the twenty years' war against France. The Regiment returned home in July 1814, having gained three further battle honours, and were awarded a fourth, "Peninsula", for their overall participation in the campaign which Napoleon referred to as his Spanish ulcer. Although not on the continent for the brief resumption of the war which was finally ended at the battle of Waterloo, the 3rd spent the second half of 1815 in Paris as part of the Army of Occupation.

6th Dragoon Guards

Recruiting in Ireland resulted rapidly in the Regiment becoming largely Irish in composition, as far as the other ranks were concerned; the 3rd Horse remained in Ireland, on garrison duty and acting as mounted policemen, for the next thirty years. Their regimental strength was reduced to twenty soldiers per troop, in the interests of economy rather than efficiency, but there seems to be no evidence that their duties in Ireland necessitated a larger complement. All the government in London was really concerned about as regards Ireland was that it should remain peaceful, by force if necessary, and not represent a realistic springboard for a French invasion of the mainland. Except at times of widespread civil disobedience, the Irish posting was a fairly relaxed one for officers and men, with the result that discipline became slack, officers frequently absenting themselves for long periods or seeking refuge from boredom in alcohol, and when the Dublin garrison erupted into near mutiny in 1765 the 3rd Horse was one of the few units to remain uninfected.

Regiments posted to Ireland were paid less than those based in England or Scotland, probably because the cost of living was cheaper, and this lower standard of pay was reflected in the price charged for officers' commissions. Prior to 1870, and except in the Artillery and Engineers, most officers had to buy their commissions and their promotions. The difference between the price of a commission or promotion in a Regiment of Horse between mainland Britain and Ireland was of the order of about £400-£500; a cornet's (or second lieutenant's) commission in the 3rd Horse in 1767 would have cost £1,067 instead of £1,600 because the Regiment was stationed in Ireland. Multiplication by about one hundred reveals the price in 1988 terms.

In 1773 Major Ralph Abercromby was appointed to command the Regiment, and did so until 1781, when he was given the colonelcy of the 103rd Regiment (or King's Irish Infantry), a hastily-raised regiment called into existence by the American Revolutionary War. Abercromby was one of Scotland's most distinguished soldiers, and one of several Scots who rose to high rank during the war against Revolutionary France. He died while in command of the British Army in the Mediterranean, of wounds received at the Battle of Alexandria in 1801. From 1756 until 1762 he had served in the 3rd Dragoon Guards, transferring to the Carabiniers as a captain in the latter year.

The American War resulted in the Carabiniers being slightly enlarged but, as with the 3rd Dragoon Guards, they remained away from the fighting as part of the forces in Ireland that were put on alert after France's entry into the war in 1778.

In 1788 the four remaining Regiments of Horse were converted to Dragoons, but with the title of Dragoon Guards. As with the experience of the 3rd Dragoon Guards in 1746, all soldiers' pay dropped in consequence – since Dragoons were not "proper" cavalry, and while officers were given a lump sum or "bounty", in mitigation, other ranks were given the choice of a discharge or a two-guinea bounty. The 3rd Horse thus became the "6th Regiment of Dragoon Guards (or Carabiniers)", a title which it retained until 1922. The size of the Regiment was specified as twenty other ranks for each of the six troops. Of these, one man in each troop was dismounted. Each troop was headed by a captain, with a lieutenant and a cornet, and the colonel, lieutenant-colonel and major each commanded a troop with the dual rank of captain. Each troop had a quartermaster, and the permanent staff was completed by an adjutant, chaplain and surgeon.

The Regiment remained at this small size until 1793 when, as a result of the likelihood of war with France, its establishment was enlarged to three hundred and seventy-two NCOs and men. Two additional troops were formed from specially-recruited soldiers of a minimum height of five feet six inches, mounted upon smaller horses than the rest of the Regiment. These were intended to serve as light cavalry in the coming campaign, and one of the troops was commanded by

Captain Stapleton Cotton, later Field Marshal Viscount Combermere. The Carabiniers landed at Ostend in November 1793 and, after wintering with the 3rd Dragoon Guards in Ghent, joined in the advance towards the French border in April 1794. They were not involved at the battle of Beaumont, but joined the 3rd and other cavalry units at Willems before enduring one of the coldest recorded winters in quarters near Bremen. The Carabiniers returned to England in 1796 and were involved in suppressing riots in Sheffield and the north-east before returning to Ireland in September 1796.

In the late 1790s Ireland was one of the few areas within the sovereignty of King George III which actually justified Westminster's fears about the likelihood of a revolutionary uprising and, in consequence, its garrisons were strengthened. The French were, of course, well aware of the potential that Ireland represented as a base for an attack on Britain itself, and so formulated a plan to invade Ireland and, with the help of the reported thousands of potentially revolutionary Irish, take over the country. The Irish rebellion, which had been smouldering for the years since the Fall of the Bastille had awoken dreams of revolution in the minds of many, finally burst into flame in May 1798. Principally involving the disenfranchised Catholic population, it was resisted to varying degrees by corps of volunteers and by the regular troops stationed in Ireland. The French invasion force landed in August and advanced inland, so badly frightening Lieutenant George de Passow of the Carabiniers that he fled the sixty miles to Athlone, taking his soldiers with him and leaving a body of militia to their fate. Notwithstanding this uncharacteristic action by a Carabinier officer, the French invasion fizzled out shortly afterwards and de Passow quietly resigned his commission.

The remainder of the war, until the truce of 1802 unwisely known as the Peace of Amiens, saw the Carabiniers continuing garrison duties in Ireland. At the resumption of hostilities in 1803 the Regiment moved to England and was enlarged to eight troops of six hundred and forty men. The following year two further troops were added, this rapid augmentation being in direct reaction to the threat of imminent invasion from France.

In 1807 four of the Carabiniers' troops were sent to South America to participate in one of the least-known campaigns of the Napoleonic Wars. Spain was then at war with Britain, not having yet been alienated by Napoleon's actions *vis-à-vis* its King, and its possessions in Argentina were seen as a rich prize. A badly thought-out expedition had been mounted from the newly-captured Cape of Good Hope in 1806. It had lined its pockets with the spoils from the treasuries of Buenos Aires and Montevideo but then got into difficulties. The four troops of the Carabiniers were part of a reinforcing Army sent out to relieve the first

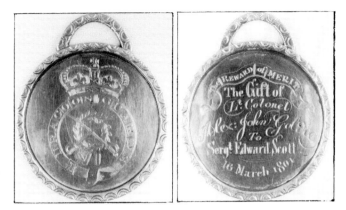

Silver regimental medal The Reward of Merit, *6th Dragoon Guards, 1801. Presented by Lieutenant-Colonel Alexander Goldie to Sergeant Edward Scott. In the days before the issue by government of Long Service and Good Conduct Medals, engraved silver medals such as these were common as regimental rewards for good conduct, for individual acts of gallantry or for skill at arms. Unhallmarked*

invasion force and they fought on foot during the campaign, which was a costly and dispiriting failure. Having decided, after considerable losses, not to try and retake Buenos Aires, the Army fell back on Montevideo and disembarked for Britain via the Cape.

The Carabiniers took no part as a regiment in the Peninsular War of 1808-14 but remained in garrisons throughout Britain, passing the period 1801-13 in Scotland. In 1813 they moved again to Ireland and sixteen men were detached for service in the Cavalry Staff Corps under Wellington in Spain. In 1812 the cocked hats worn by the Regiment were exchanged for leather helmets ornamented with brass, and this pattern of helmet, the first of many to be worn by the Carabiniers, continued in service until 1818. The establishment of the Regiment varied as the fortunes of the war changed, and on return to Scotland from Ireland after Waterloo in July 1815 the peacetime strength was fixed at five hundred and forty-four officers and men.

Royal Scots Greys

The Greys stayed in Scotland less than a year, and from 1764 until 1769 were stationed in various parts of England, returning to Scotland in 1769. They then returned to England in 1770 and were posted about the country on a number of different duties until 1783 when, again briefly, Scotland became their base. In common with all other regiments, recruiting was not at this time restricted to specific areas, and it is recorded that the Greys were, as a matter of policy, not averse to including non-Scots in their ranks, assuming of course that the recruits were up to scratch. In common with other cavalry regiments, the Regiment's duties were primarily those of mounted policemen at a time when no other form of nationally-organised police existed.

In 1768 they were ordered to change their cloth embroidered "mitre" caps for fur caps, but appear to have successfully resisted this innovation until 1777. The fur cap, predecessor of the modern bearskin cap, was confined to fusiliers and grenadiers (élite troops) among the infantry, and the Greys appear to have been the only cavalry of the line to have been allowed to wear such a head-dress. The adoption of the tall cap and the use of the flaming grenade as a badge both indicate that the Regiment was regarded, by whoever authorised these sartorial embellishments, as an élite Regiment. It is doubly unfortunate, therefore, that no record exists of the reason why these differentiations were made to the Regiment's uniform.

In 1778 the Regiment's strength was increased and a detachment of ninety-six NCOs and men ordered to be dressed, equipped and trained as light cavalry. The following year these soldiers, together with others similarly trained from three other Dragoon regiments, were separated from their parent regiments and formed into a separate regiment of light cavalry, the 21st (Light) Dragoons.

More postings around England followed the return from Scotland in 1784, and the outbreak of war with France in 1793 found the Greys in Lancashire. In July 1793 four of the Regiment's nine troops landed at Ostend while the five remaining troops were increased to eighty men each. After wintering in Ghent the Army, including the four Greys troops, began campaigning again in April 1794. At the Battle of Willems in May 1794 the four troops of the regiment were in the forefront of the action when the British cavalry charged into and broke several squares of French infantry; leading the attack on one of the broken squares was an officer of the Greys whose name, regrettably, has not been recorded. To break an infantry square by means other than concentrated artillery fire was almost unheard-of and involved, in this case, the officer jumping his horse over three ranks of soldiers, surviving the experience and then making a gap large enough for his troopers to get in and hack, chop, slash and slice around them. Nothing similar would happen again until the last years of the Napoleonic Wars.

The Greys detachment returned to Britain in 1795 and remained in England on garrison duties, and as potential resisters of invasion, until 1807. A detachment of the Regiment was present at the funeral of Admiral Lord Nelson in 1806, and the Regiment's establishment fluctuated as the chances of action advanced or receded. From 1796 until his death in Egypt in 1801, the Colonel of the Regiment was General Sir Ralph Abercromby, one of the few occasions when the service of a single individual has linked all the then separate components of the present Regiment.

The Greys took no part in the Peninsular War but were stationed in Scotland for eighteen months from January 1807, and in Ireland for two years from 1808.

Ram's horn snuff mull, The Gift of Lieutt. Alexr. Campbell to the Mess of the Officers of the RNB Dragoons 1806.
Snuff-taking was a custom among men from the seventeenth to the twentieth centuries but has now largely disappeared. Mulls such as this, which contained several ounces in the compartment under the lid, would have been for use on the Mess table after dinner and would be circulated much as boxes of cigars and cigarettes are today.

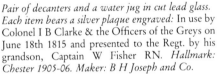

Pair of decanters and a water jug in cut lead glass. Each item bears a silver plaque engraved: In use by Colonel I B Clarke & the Officers of the Greys on June 18th 1815 and presented to the Regt. by his grandson, Captain W Fisher RN. *Hallmark: Chester 1905-06. Maker: B H Joseph and Co.*

Although the war affected the civilian population far less than did the two world wars of the twentieth century, the war years were a time of considerable privation for the poor, of high taxes, of conscription to the militia and press-ganging to the Navy, and of a gradual feeling of resentment among the industrialised towns at the way in which they were largely unrepresented in Parliament. Thus, although the Greys remained at home, there was sufficient civilian unrest to make their presence, and that of other regiments similarly stationed, necessary for the maintenance of what passed at that time for law and order. Service in the militia became compulsory after 1802 and was very unpopular indeed, principally because it often led to drafting into regular infantry regiments fighting in Spain, but also because it involved service away from home and family. The concept of a population patriotically united behind a wartime government did not apply across the board in the Britain of the Napoleonic Wars, and the use of soldiers to enforce unpopular laws was a common-place. No records of the Greys having to drag civilians from their houses and into barracks exist, but it is likely that all regiments stationed in Britain at the time had unpopular duties to perform.

Scotland for ever! A depiction of the 2nd (Royal North British) Dragoons at full charge in line during the charge of the Union Brigade, Waterloo, 1815. Like many other depictions of the action, it is stylised and inaccurate; unlike many others, it is immensely powerful and striking. The artist, who finished this painting in 1881, was the wife of an army officer and had encountered the Greys on manoeuvres at Aldershot, where she had sketched them charging. The last of her more popular paintings, Scotland for ever! inspired many other versions, none of which captured the spirit of the original. Artist: Elizabeth, Lady Butler (1846-1933)

Thus, when Napoleon escaped from Elba in 1815 and threatened again to disrupt the newly-won peace of Europe, the Regiment had seen no active service for twenty years. Probably because of this, amongst other reasons of course, it was raring to go. Its strength was doubled to nearly one thousand officers and men, and six of the ten troops were put in a state of readiness for immediate embarkation. The order to move was received on 6 April and the six troops of the Regiment commanded by Lieutenant-Colonel James Hamilton arrived in Ostend on 19 April, having crossed from Bristol to Gravesend in seven days. The Greys were brigaded with two other regiments of Dragoons, the 1st (Royals) -now part of the Blues and Royals – and the 6th (Inniskilling) – now part of the 5th Royal Inniskilling Dragoon Guards. The title of the Brigade was the Union Brigade, symbolic of the link between England (the Royals), Scotland (the Greys) and Ireland (the Inniskillings).

Much of the rest of April, and the whole of May, was spent in quarters of changing location and varying quality, while Wellington attempted to discover what Napoleon's intentions were. That an attack in the form of an eastward thrust was imminent was not in question, but its direction and strength were, and little

Silver table centrepiece of Sergeant Charles Ewart with the standard and eagle of the 45th French Infantry. Presented to the Royal Scots Greys in memory of Lt.-Col. Sir Alfred Welby, commanding 1892-96, by his wife and son. *Clearly derived in pose from the painting* The Fight for the Standard *by Richard Ansdell, this centrepiece depicts Ewart, having taken the standard, in the act of cutting down a French lancer in order to retain it.* Hallmark: London 1886-87. Maker: Stephen Smith and Son

could be planned or achieved until some indication of the position, strength and plans of the French Army was ascertained. First British blood was drawn at Quatre Bras on 15 June and Napoleon's route became obvious: a thrust at Brussels to end matters quickly and to drive the Allied armies back into the sea. The Greys were called forward to Quatre Bras but arrived after the action and bivouacked in the fields. Retreat in the face of powerful French forces followed for the next couple of days until, in appalling weather, the Army made camp south of Waterloo.

The battle which followed, on 18 June 1815, established the course of European history for a century and was of such importance to the growth of British power that it rapidly took on the status of a semi-mythical event, especially for those who were not there. For the Greys it was a slaughter, a baptism of fire after two

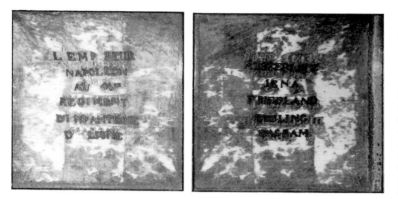

The standard of the 45th French Infantry, captured by Sergeant Charles Ewart, 2nd (Royal North British) Dragoons, at Waterloo 1815. Essentially a fringed Tricouleur, the standard was issued to the regiment in 1815 after Napoleon's escape from Elba, with sufficient letters and numbers for their title and battle honours to be sewn to the surface.

decades of relative peace, the event which made them a household name and the battle at which they captured their most treasured and revered possession. There are almost as many accounts of the battle as there were participants in it, and there are, it is thought, still Frenchmen who believe that they won. Wellington had a low regard for the British cavalry since it had, as he put it, got him into several "scrapes" in the Peninsular campaign by its tendency to charge off hither and yon and become ungovernable after achieving its object of smashing, demoralising and sabreing the enemy. As an experienced rider to hounds, with a healthy mixture of Irish and West Country blood, Wellington knew only too well how the exhilaration afforded by a mad thrash across country could easily overwhelm the better judgment of even the most staid of his cavalry commanders, the staid ones being a rarity, and so he tended to use his cavalry when it could only do good and not get itself into mischief. Waterloo, though, was not a Peninsular battle; there were no fortified positions – no lines of Torres Vedras – to retreat to in good order. Wellington knew that, with the sea at his back, this was a battle on which he had to gamble everything and risk losing all. And he could not afford to lose. Fortunately, he had battle-hardened troops from the Peninsula, who had faced the French before and become used to thrashing them, and eager fresh troops from home, anxious to prove themselves and to get a slice of the action before it was too late. He was also facing an ill-formed army that was over-stretched and under-supplied – staking everything on a last extravagant throw of the dice.

The Greys went into the battle three hundred and ninety-one strong; by the evening one hundred and two of them were dead and ninety-eight were wounded. These figures reversed the usual ratio of killed to wounded and may be explained by the nature of the Regiment's part in the battle. Formed up on the reverse slope of a ridge (in order to be invisible to the greater part of the French Army), the Regiment had had to wait for several hours since the opening moves of the battle had been made. In front of them were the infantry of the 9th Brigade within the 5th Division, and the battalions within this Brigade were facing down the slope

The Fight for the Standard. *A depiction of Sergeant Charles Ewart, having taken the standard from the standard-bearer of the 45th French Infantry, defending his prize from recapture by a French lancer. Painted in 1847, a year after Ewart's death, this massive canvas, approximately 11' x 9', is a highly romanticised view of Ewart as the noble Victorian hero. Artist: Richard Ansdell (1815-1885)*

towards the masses of French infantry, advancing in columns across the valley and up the slope. The Brigade was ordered to open fire, and did so with great effect, the volleys of musket balls tearing bloody swathes through the French soldiers. Volley after volley shook and staggered the columns, yet they kept coming, so the Union and Household Brigades were ordered forward to lend their weight to the argument. The effect of these regiments of heavy cavalry charging down the slope and full tilt into the massed ranks of the French can be imagined. The two French Divisions commanded by Donzelot and Marcognet, within the 1st Infantry Corps of the French Armée du Nord commanded by General Jean Drouet, Comte d'Erlon, were cut to pieces or trampled by the wielded steel and thundering horseflesh of the Union Brigade and Household Brigade (Life Guards and Royal Horse Guards). Two French standards, only recently given to the 45th and 105th Regiments of Infantry by the newly-returned Emperor, and topped with their glittering gilded eagles, were taken by the Royals and the Greys.

Sergeant Charles Ewart relieved the 45th Infantry of its rallying-point early in

Saddle used by Lieutenant James Gape at the Battle of Waterloo 1815, together with a contemporary valise. Gape, who joined the Regiment in 1813, was narrowly missed by two musket balls which damaged and lodged in his saddle. He retired from the Regiment as a captain in 1833.

Items associated with Ensign Charles Ewart: the sword reputed to have been carried by him at Waterloo; his Waterloo Medal; a watch bought by him in Paris during the occupation; and a silver snuffbox presented to him by Mr Henry Brown in 1827 and inscribed on the base, From Henry Brown to his friend Mr Ewart, an offering to valour.

the engagement and cut down two other French soldiers as well as the standard-bearer in order to keep his prize, which he was ordered to take to the rear before rejoining the Regiment. Ewart was an expert swordsman, at a period when strength with the sword was more important than grace or skill, and adept at handling an ugly, badly-balanced, poor quality weapon which was little use when used at the point or thrust and scarcely better at cutting; that he managed to use it with such frequent and terminal effect speaks more for the strength of his arms, shoulders and back than for the efficiency of his weapon. He had already spoilt the day of a decidedly unchivalrous French officer by the time he got stuck into the standard-bearer of the 45th. This bad-mannered Frenchman had had his life spared by Ewart on the request of Cornet Francis Kinchant at the beginning of the action but had then, when Ewart's back was turned, pistolled Kinchant in gratitude. Hearing the shot and seeing his officer fall, Ewart had an understandable sense of humour failure and promptly decapitated the Frenchman. In later years Ewart referred to his capture of the eagle but seldom, and always with unfailing modesty, giving the impression that he was far prouder of the summary justice dealt to an enemy who had shown such a poor grasp of good manners.

Ewart's move to the rear with his captured standard and eagle may well have saved his life and preserved the trophy for the Regiment. As he was trotting rebelliously to the rear – having been ordered so to do by the Brigade commander – the Greys swept onward into the valley, cutting, slashing and cheering, and up

Scotland yet, on to victory! A depiction of the 2nd (Royal North British) Dragoons charging through the 92nd (Gordon) Highlanders at the Battle of Waterloo, 1815, and into the advancing French infantry. Painted in 1904, this is one of the many depictions of the action which lent credence to the story of the "Gordons and Greys stirrup charge". Artist: Richard Caton Woodville (1856-1927)

the facing slope through a field battery of French cannon – whose gunners were given short shrift – far further than they should have advanced. As a result, the horses became quite blown and the Regiment unable to rally, escape quickly or properly defend itself when it was fallen upon in revenge for its slaughter by the 6th and 9th Cuirassiers of Farine's Brigade of Cavalry. Attempting to return through the now largely disabled guns of the French artillery, the Regiment was attacked in the flank by the 4th Lancers and seriously cut up. Lieutenant-Colonel Hamilton, commanding the Regiment, was wounded in both arms and attempted to lead the Greys out of the action while holding the reins in his teeth; he was soon shot dead.

Amazingly, a remnant of the Greys survived the action and, temporarily brigaded with the Life Guards, repeatedly attacked French infantry positions on occasions during the remainder of the battle. As the tide began to turn in Wellington's favour, as the Imperial Guard were broken by the fire of the Foot Guards and as Napoleon turned to flee, so the surviving Regiment joined in the

Ram's horn snuff mull, mounted in brass, with a copper badge and tools. Inscribed: Sgt. Anderson's horn, R.N.B. Dn. F. Troop. *Reputed to have been recovered from the field of Waterloo after the battle.*

pursuit to end the matter.

As memories of the horror of the battle faded, and as its glories became magnified in the telling and by the passage of years, so the stories began. As Britain grew stronger, largely as a result of the defeat of France at Waterloo, so the true historical significance of the battle began to be appreciated and one of its most famous episodes, the charge of the Scots Greys, became a subject for artists and myth-makers. Historical accuracy is the first casualty in the pursuit of romance and, while the friendly link that has bound the Greys and the Gordon Highlanders so closely over the years is to be valued, there is no doubt that the 92nd never rode into action at Waterloo hanging onto the stirrup-leathers of the Greys. It is probable that many Gordons were trampled or knocked over as the Regiment rode through the 92nd in their eagerness to get at the French. Of far greater interest and significance remain the sword said to have been used at Waterloo by Charles Ewart and the bullet-holed saddle that bore Lieutenant James Gape into action and out again on 18 June 1815.

The Regiment remained in France for the remainder of 1815 as part of the Army of Occupation and Sergeant Charles Ewart was commissioned Ensign Ewart in a battalion of veterans as a reward for capturing the eagle that was ordered to be borne, in facsimile, on the guidons and other relevant appointments of the Greys.

CHAPTER THREE

A Long Peace and a Short War

1816-1856

3rd Dragoon Guards

The period of fractionally less than forty years between the defeat of Napoleon at Waterloo and the beginning of the Crimean War has been known to British historians for more than a century as the Long Peace. This phrase reflects the fact that Britain was not at war with any other power in Europe during the period. It ignores an earlier time of European peace between 1763 and 1793 and a later, and longer, one between 1856 and 1899 but, despite these anomalies, the phrase has stuck, even if its adhesion has weakened. The British Government conducted campaigns of Imperial expansion in India and southern Africa during this time, utilising either its own troops or those of the East India Company, but none involved the regiments which are the subject of this book.

If all was officially peaceful in terms of Britain's European foreign policy for the four decades after Waterloo, the position was very different at home for much of the time. The Industrial Revolution had gained momentum in the years since the end of the eighteenth century and, although it made Britain the leading industrial power in Europe until the middle of the nineteenth century, its effects on the country's social fabric were far-reaching and traumatic. Industrialisation created new cities where only villages had been, and removed work from hands in order to give it to machines. Rural areas suffered first depression and then depopulation as, increasingly, manufacturing was centralised; widespread unemployment and poverty followed. Life was cheap, capital punishment and transportation were the norm for major and minor offences and widespread civil unrest was so common as to be predictable. Organised resistance to industrialisation occurred sporadically throughout the first two decades of the nine-teenth century, the societies which stage-managed it being known as the Luddites after a frame-breaker of the eighteenth century. These pressures combined with failed harvests, rising prices and clamour for electoral reform, until British society appeared to be on the brink of revolution. Between the excesses of the mob and the legislators stood the Army and, for regiments stationed at home between Waterloo and the Crimea, a principal task was the maintenance or restoration of law and order. Cavalry regiments were ideally suited to the task: in giving evidence to the Finance Commission in 1828 the Duke of Wellington – although never an entirely enthusiastic supporter of the mounted arm – said:

> It is much more desirable to employ cavalry for the purposes of police than infantry; for this reason: cavalry inspires more terror at the same time that it does much less mischief. A body of 20 or 30 Horse will disperse a mob with the utmost facility, whereas 400 or 500 infantry will not effect the same object without the use of their firearms, and a great deal of mischief may be done.

Cavalry could do mischief of course, especially when they were yeomanry – part-time cavalry drawn from those sectors of rural society least likely to contain sympathisers with the grievances of an urban mob, or poorly-disciplined urban tradesmen with the same prejudices. Occasions such as the "Peterloo massacre" of 1819 in Manchester are well recorded and appal far more now than they did at the time simply because such occasions of mob-dispersal by violent means were frequent and rarely thought of as unusual or excessive.

Cavalry regiments, because of their role as mounted police, rarely served united anywhere in Britain or Ireland but were split up into troops or half-troops throughout widespread districts; their presence, it was felt, acting as a discouragement to orchestrated mob violence. Thus, when the 3rd Dragoon Guards returned from a France newly enjoying the benefits of a restored monarchy in January 1816, they were immediately reduced to a peacetime establishment and posted to southern Yorkshire for six months before sailing for Ireland, where their strength was further reduced. The Regiment remained in Ireland until 1820, after which it passed two years in south-west Scotland – based in the trouble-spots of Hamilton, Paisley and Glasgow, where industrial unrest was common. In 1821 the lowest of peacetime establishments was fixed at six troops containing 362 officers and men with 253 horses, it rarely being possible or necessary to mount the entire Regiment. During their time in Scotland the Regiment was united for the visit of King George IV to Edinburgh in 1822. The King landed at the port of Leith and the Regiment formed part of his guard of honour, later being reviewed by him on the sands at Musselburgh – a favourite place for Scottish reviews because of its size, accessibility from Edinburgh and agreeable position. Two

Silver, lidded tankard. Presented by William Henry Wilson to the Head Quarters Mess of his former regiment, The Prince of Wales Dragoon Guards, Feb. 27th 1843. *Hallmark: London 1765-66. Makers: William and James Priest.*

Silver, lidded tankard. Presented to the Mess of the 3rd Dragoon Guards by the Officers of F Troop, Augt. 15th 1846; Captn. Garratt, Lieut. Marsh, Cornet Oakes. *Hallmark: Newcastle 1752-53. Maker: James or John Kirkup*

further years followed in northern England, after which the period 1824-28 was spent in Ireland. In 1828 the Regiment returned to Scotland for one year, and from there moved to the English Midlands and then to the West Country.

As a form of economic stability gradually returned after the war, so the pressure for reform of the electoral system grew, especially from those disenfranchised by the existing system. The method of electing Members of Parliament had not kept pace with the changing nature of Britain during the Industrial Revolution and so, among many other abuses and anomalies, formerly thriving communities retained their Member – while being themselves moribund – and the new industrial centres of the Midlands and north remained proportionately unrepresented. Elections in Britain, throughout the eighteenth century and before any prospect of a universal franchise loomed, were often riotous affairs with nepotism and peculation running neck and neck, with the mob, rural as well as urban, frequently enlisted – while largely disenfranchised – to intimidate the few voters. Universal male suffrage was not to come to Britain until 1868, and so the widespread disturbances which preceded the passing of the First Reform Bill in 1832 largely involved masses of people who were never intended to benefit from the Bill's inception.

One of the worst pre-Reform riots took place in Bristol in 1831 and directly involved the Regiment, hence this excursion into political history. The Recorder of the City of Bristol, Sir Charles Wetherall, was vociferously opposed to any Parliamentary reform

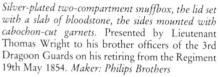

Silver-plated two-compartment snuffbox, the lid set with a slab of bloodstone, the sides mounted with cabochon-cut garnets. Presented by Lieutenant Thomas Wright to his brother officers of the 3rd Dragoon Guards on his retiring from the Regiment 19th May 1854. *Maker: Philips Brothers*

and so, when he arrived at the city in October 1831 to open the Assizes, his presence was sufficient to provide an excuse for anarchy. Special constables were sworn in and three troops of cavalry, two of the 14th Light Dragoons and one of the 3rd Dragoon Guards, were placed in readiness for some excitement. Crowd control in the 1830s was little different to that practised against rioters today, even allowing for the slight change in the value of life. The 14th were pelted with anything peltable, tempers frayed and people got hurt – on both sides. Restraint on the troops' part was tempered by incompetent and vacillatory leadership from the senior officer, a half-pay lieutenant-colonel called Brereton, who refused to issue direct orders or to take responsibility. The Mansion House was sacked, two gaols burnt to the ground and other public buildings set alight in a frenzy of drunken destruction. The 14th were sent away by Brereton, who was clearly not up to the task, and Captain William Warrington of the 3rd Dragoon Guards was unable to get cogent or lucid instructions from his superior officer; he refused to act without them. When, eventually, both Brereton and one of the few magistrates who could be prised from beneath his bed arrived and sanctioned the use of force, the 3rd Dragoon Guards troop trotted into Queen Square, part of which was ablaze and most of which was full of swaying, pugnacious rioters, and proceeded to lay about them with their swords. Being too few in number to effect much, they held the balance until the 14th could be recalled, who, aided by a couple of troops of the North Somerset Yeomanry, sabred the mob with alacrity and cleared the streets in a matter of a few hours. Casualties were considerable and recriminations inevitable. Both Brereton and Warrington were court-martialled, the latter being allowed to retire by sale of his commission on account of poor health: the penalty of caution overriding initiative. Brereton shot himself during the course of the trial, but not before it was recorded by a local artist, Rolinda Sharples, on a large canvas which now decorates the walls of Bristol's City Art Gallery and which owes much to the artist's capacity as an eager-to-please portrait painter.

Silver, lidded tankard, the Corinthian Cup. Won by Wartnaby at the Kildare Hunt Races 1855. Presented by Major Carlyon to the Mess of the 3rd Dragoon Guards. *Hallmark: London 1704-05. Maker unidentified*

For the next twenty-five years, during which civil unrest continued little abated by the Reform Bill but fuelled by widespread economic deprivation, the 3rd Dragoon Guards continued to be stationed throughout Britain and Ireland. Between 1834 and 1837 the Regiment was dispersed by troops throughout Ireland, although based in Dublin. The following six years were spent in Scotland and England before returning to Ireland in 1843, to an island fast in the grip of famine and experiencing hardship and misery to an extent unknown on the mainland. In 1846 the Regiment returned to Scotland and remained in the central Lowland belt for two years, during which it was called out to act in aid of magistrates in Glasgow and Hamilton. If the 1820s had been the decade of Reform riots, the 1830s and 1840s were those of Chartism, a widespread if disconnected movement convinced that a charter of civil rights and liberties was long overdue. Chartist meetings were vast and frequently peaceful, but occasionally broke up into riots which necessitated special constables and soldiers, the presence and conduct of whom frequently – if unintentionally – exacerbated the situation. Chartism in Britain and famine in Ireland were compounded in 1848 by fears of domestic revolution spread from across the Channel where France, Austria, Prussia and the other apparently settled states were infected one by one with the cry for parliamentary government, for reform, and for redress of grievances; all the things which led to barricades, to firing squads and to semblances of democracy. Although Britain remained unaffected, the Government was far from complacent about its ability to survive, and all the regiments at home were involved in actively cowing their countrymen. Between 1848 and 1852 the Regiment was stationed in and around Sheffield, a new industrial town with supposedly great potential for mischief, before returning to Ireland to supervise elections. The Regiment remained in Ireland throughout the Crimean War of 1854-56, sending 105 volunteers to serve in other regiments and training men and horses to supply reinforcements.

6th Dragoon Guards

The role of the Carabiniers during the Long Peace was little different to that of the 3rd Dragoon Guards, and their stations changed as the political climate fluctuated. From Scotland in 1816, the Regiment moved to Lancashire in 1817 and further south, into the west Midlands and Welsh borders, the following year.

Concepts of training were restricted chiefly to field days during this period, grand reviews where regiments would go through clean, tidy and heavily stylised mock battles consisting of much charging about, wheeling by troop and general equitation aimed more at delighting spectators than at schooling soldiers for the realities either of war or of crowd control.

The traditionally separate natures of light and heavy cavalry continued to obtain: the light cavalry for skirmishing, reconnaissance and other duties requiring speed above all; the heavy cavalry retained for the shock effect of the mass charge. By the end of the Long Peace, though, the distinction between roles had blurred considerably and, as was to be demonstrated during the Crimean War, both light and heavy cavalry were able to master and effect the charge.

As has been said, the campaigns fought in India and Africa during the Long Peace affected neither of the Dragoon Guards regiments dealt with here. Such campaigning was left to the light cavalry of the mounted arm, either that of the Crown or that of the East India Company. The Company possessed several light cavalry regiments within the armies that it maintained in the three presidencies of Bengal, Madras and Bombay and these, together with the Crown's Light Dragoon, Hussar or Lancer regiments, were ideally suited to campaigning outside Europe. Their suitability was measured principally on the grounds of stature, both of men and of horses. Light cavalry troopers were traditionally slighter in build than their heavy counterparts, and their horses were smaller and nimbler too. Since, for the most part, regiments did not take their horses with them on postings to India or Africa, any more than today's cavalry regiments take their tanks back and forth between Salisbury Plain and Germany, heavy cavalry could not be posted outside Europe because the mounts which would await them would be unequal to the task of carrying the soldiers. As, however, the distinction between light and heavy cavalry began to blur, so regiments of Dragoon Guards became more frequent visitors to the sub-continent.

A constant succession of domestic postings, little prospect of foreign adventures and the atmosphere of studied, almost decadent, gentility which gradually permeated the rather monastic, if luxurious atmosphere of the officers' mess, inevitably led to boredom, inefficiency, corruption and petty squabbling. Indeed, under the circumstances, it is remarkable that any of the Dragoon Guards regiments stationed at home during the Long Peace remained effective. The 6th suffered from ennui as much as any regiment, but one spectacular case has survived to be retold.

Lieutenant-Colonel St George French, who had commanded the Regiment since 1811, and clearly felt himself well installed and beyond either reproach or detection, was still in command when the 6th were inspected during their stay in Newcastle upon Tyne in 1820. Inspecting them was the Inspector-General of Cavalry, Major General Lord Edward Somerset, who had commanded the Household Cavalry Brigade at Waterloo. The character of such inspections depended chiefly upon the acuity of the inspector, and so it may well be either that Lord Edward was feeling more sharp than usual or that rumours that all was not well had filtered through to the Horse Guards. Certainly someone had been at work spreading alarm and despondency, because the quartermaster was arraigned before a court martial and accused of writing an anonymous letter which hinted, apparently with commendable lack of subtlety, that the paymaster was somewhat less than entirely honest. The degree to which the anonymous suggestion was accurate does not seem to have been investigated, or at least is not reported, but the quartermaster was acquitted. Even in 1820, it seems, the well-known probity and honest uprightness of quartermasters and paymasters was a difficult matter to gainsay. Colonel French, on the other hand, was called before a court martial to answer a total of six charges. These ranged from "keeping a woman in barracks", through "publicly dealing in horses", via "fraudulent conduct in the sale of a horse", to "causing the troop registers of horses to be cut and defaced". On the basis of there being no smoke without fire, one has to suspect that a small degree of accuracy may have attended a few of the charges, but French was acquitted on four of them, three of which were the last three quoted above, and found guilty on the first charge: of keeping a woman in barracks. One can speculate that this arrangement allowed him to be comfortable while horse-trading and not have to choose between forms of diversion, but, in any case, he was only sentenced to be admonished and allowed to retain command of the Carabiniers. Slightly less than a century later a distant kinsman, Field Marshal Sir John French, Lord Ypres, commanded the British Expeditionary Force during the first years of the First World War.

The following year Colonel French took the Regiment to Ireland: thirteen horses are said to have died on the passage along the Bristol Channel and across the Irish Sea. A further four were subsequently sold, apparently on account of lameness. Whether the Colonel's friend accompanied him to Ireland is not recorded.

Three years in Ireland were followed by time in Scotland, until 1826, when the

Three officer's full-dress sabretaches:
Back: 3rd Dragoon Guards c. 1827;
Front, left: 3rd Dragoon Guards c. 1835;
Front, right: 6th Dragoon Guards c. 1840.

Sabretaches are decorated pouches which were
worn hanging from slings suspended from the
waistbelt and were used for carrying dispatches.

Regiment returned to England. Separated and detached by troops, it patrolled the west Midlands and central southern England for four years until 1830, when it returned to Ireland. After a further four years the Regiment returned to Scotland until 1835, after which it passed two years in Nottingham and Brighton. Three troops of the Carabiniers were on duty in London on 28 June 1838 at the coronation of Queen Victoria, where they also took part in the Royal Review in Hyde Park a fortnight later. Further domestic duties followed for the next decade with little of any consequence being recorded.

In 1851 the Carabiniers were ordered to take a step that marked them out, when clad in full dress uniform, for the next seventy years. They were ordered to convert themselves to light cavalry, while retaining the Dragoon Guards title. Their recruits were ordered to be less than twelve stones in weight (168 pounds or 76 kilos) and the size of their mounts was proportionately reduced; this gives an idea of the weight required of heavy cavalry. The traditional colour of light cavalry uniforms was dark blue (except for a period during the reign of King William IV when they, too, adopted scarlet), and so the Carabiniers lost their scarlet coatees and had them replaced with blue ones. They retained their helmets, in keeping with their continued designation as Dragoon Guards, but adopted the double trouser-seam stripe of the light cavalry in substitution for the single broad stripe of the heavies. A laced pouch-belt with "pickers" (silver stylised arrows usually based on the prongs necessary to keep the touch-hole of the flintlock carbine free of fouling gunpowder) was adopted. Hatless, the Regiment resembled Light Dragoons; covered, they looked like the compromise they were.

Once converted, the Regiment was liable for service in India and, for several years, it awaited orders to move, orders which seemed imminent and were then countermanded as war with Russia became increasingly inevitable. While kicking its heels at home, the 6th provided a squadron, together with the band and trumpeters, to

An officer's charger, possibly that of the Commanding Officer or a troop leader, 6th Dragoon Guards 1845. The charger is attended by the officer's orderly. Two other officers and the Regiment can be seen in the background, with trumpeters and kettledrummer on the left. Artist: John Ferneley Junior (1815-1862)

form part of the immense military procession that attended the state funeral of the Duke of Wellington in 1852.

When the Crimean War eventually began in 1854 the Carabiniers were not among the initial embarkation of light and heavy cavalry regiments which formed the Light and Heavy Brigades within the Cavalry Division. Indeed, by the time that the Regiment eventually arrived in the Crimea, having sent several issues of reinforcement horses to the cavalry regiments already there, all the significant battles had been fought and the Allies had settled down in trenches before the naval base, and principal fortress of the Crimea, of Sebastopol. The Carabiniers eventually arrived on Russian soil in August 1855, having been moved out by squadrons. The squadron as a unit was used until 1868 only for active service purposes, troops being retained for administrative and peacetime use.

The Allies, French, British, Turkish and Sardinian, were well entrenched around Sebastopol, and constant reinforcements and acclimatisation, together with the blockading ability of the Royal Navy in the Black Sea, meant that they retained a large measure of control over the Crimean peninsula. The Carabiniers were employed away from Sebastopol, where cavalry was of little tactical use, in maintaining the blockade against mainland Russia and preventing any build-up of Russian strength which might threaten the Allied flanks. Skirmishing with and harassment of small Russian forces was the norm until a truce was agreed at the beginning of 1856, by which time the Regiment had returned to Scutari in Turkey. In May 1856 the Carabiniers returned to Britain and began the delayed preparations for their first passage to India. By the end of the year, travelling in four ships, the 6th Dragoon Guards had embarked for the sub-continent.

Royal Scots Greys

The four decades of peace were spent by the Greys in the same manner as that passed by the 3rd and 6th Dragoon Guards: internal security. The Regiment left the Army of Occupation in France in January 1816 and spent eighteen months in Canterbury, a traditional cavalry posting. The following year, until July 1818, was spent in Scotland, being quartered in Piershill Barracks in Edinburgh, whereupon the Greys moved to Ireland for three years. In 1821 they returned to England, spending a few weeks in the Midlands before being posted to London in July for the coronation of King George IV. In 1822 the Greys moved to Scotland and, with the 3rd Dragoon Guards, were in attendance upon the King during his visit to Scotland in that year. Leaving Scotland in 1823, the Regiment moved gradually southwards through England for the next four years in a variety of postings from Carlisle to Ipswich. Between 1827 and 1830 it was stationed in Ireland and, on return, was posted to the West Country before moving to south-east England in November 1830.

Southern England, particularly the rural areas, was in turmoil during the early 1830s, not exclusively on the question of Reform, but rather to do with rising prices, falling wages, failed harvests and social misery in a society devoid of a system of welfare other than the workhouse. Farmers were blamed by sections of the rural poor who formed secret societies similar to those which had existed in Ireland since the middle of the eighteenth century and which were less interested in redress of grievances than in seeking revenge; ricks were burnt, animals disabled, farmers' families threatened. The societies were noted for their threatening messages usually signed "Swing" or "Captain Swing", which would be left pinned to farmhouse doors or to hamstrung cattle, and which were deliberately redolent of a lynch-mob atmosphere. Many of those in rural communities who were not directly implicated in the disturbances knew better than to inform on their neighbours who were, and the task of the authorities, aided by the soldiers, in attempting to eradicate the rioting was consequently made difficult. In some villages the sight of a trooper in a red coat was enough to send villagers scurrying for cover, although in others the soldiers were seen as protectors of lives and properties.

One of the most illuminating, if highly subjective, accounts of soldiering in the Greys in the 1830s was published in 1848. The autobiography of Alexander Somerville devotes fully a third of its length to the period from 1831 to 1832 when Somerville was a trooper in the Greys, at the centre of a highly-publicised military enquiry following a flogging, and something of a figurehead for the vociferous supporters of the Reform movement. "Somerville the Scots Grey" was a cry throughout Britain for the supporters of Reform. They, seeing in this apparently unjustly – and savagely – punished trooper a victim symbolic both of the rights of the common man and the anti-Reform nature of the establishment (as represented by an exclusive and aristocratic cavalry regiment whose officers appeared to be beyond the law), took Somerville up, protested his case in Parliament and used him, quite

An unidentified regimental officer, 6th Dragoon Guards 1851-1855. The sitter wears the blue Light Dragoon uniform adopted in 1851 and worn in this style until 1855. Artist: L Poyet (1798-1873)

Silver snuffbox with a gilded interior, the weighted lid decorated with the reverse of the Waterloo Medal 1815, a profile of the Prince Regent and martial trophies. Presented by Cornet Thomas Walker to the Officers of the Royal North British Dragoons, 15th April 1818 *Hallmark: Edinburgh 1817-18 Maker: Richard Haxton*

deliberately, for political purposes. Notwithstanding the detail of the political side of the Reform movement, Somerville's autobiography contains fascinating insights into the working of the Regiment for this brief period when it was the centre of such unwelcome publicity.

That he was intelligent, articulate and literate there is no doubt. Indeed, Somerville makes the point, nobly for a Scot, that one of the reasons why the exploits of the Highlanders during the Napoleonic Wars are so well known is that, unlike their English or Irish comrades, they could – and did – write letters home, which were frequently published in local newspapers. Somerville was born in the Lammermuir Hills in 1811 and began flirting with the idea of being a soldier in his late teens. Imminent starvation decided him that little alternative existed, and he was enlisted by a corporal in Edinburgh High Street, a corporal then bemoaning a short-lived Army regulation which had deprived him of his moustache. Once enlisted and examined, by the garrison surgeon in the Castle, Somerville and his fellow recruits left from Leith for London by sea. They spent two weeks in London awaiting an escort to take them to the Regiment in Brighton, not being trusted – despite repeated pleas – to make their own way there, and they eventually set out on foot in January 1832. After a two-day journey they arrived, were relieved of their clothes, which were in theory burnt (but were probably sold to one of the many old-clothes dealers who were among the many types of optimistic parasite who frequented barracks), and were placed in the hospital to treat, by the most rudimentary methods, a soldier with cholera. Cholera was a new disease and excited panic. Having come from Scotland, where an epidemic was raging, Somerville and his fellow recruits were suspected of carrying the disease and were placed in a kind of quarantine with the one soldier in the Regiment who had contracted it. The victim, Trooper James Miller – servant to Cornet Lachlan Macquarie – eventually recovered, more by luck than good nursing, and after a fortnight Somerville was allowed to begin the process of becoming a Scots Grey. He was measured for his uniform and his boots and issued with his kit. From his enlistment bounty of £2.12.6d (£2.62½) he received ten shillings (50p), the rest going to pay on account for his uniform and kit. The remaining sum owed, £3.10s (£3.50), would be gradually stopped out of his pay until the debt was settled.

The Regiment was ordered to Birmingham, Somerville and the other recruits not yet trained to ride, marching with the baggage train. His almost lyrical account of the march across the rural England of 1832 evokes not-too-distant folk memories of unspoilt villages, dusty roads and apple-cheeked, smocked country people. His account of the Regiment's reception in village inns or the public houses where the soldiers were billeted underlines not only the gastronomic differences between Scotland and southern England, but also how well-fed the Army was when on the march in England. He tasted roast beef and apple puddings for the first time in Horsham, roast goose for the first time in Thame, and was introduced to Yorkshire pudding in Warwick.

Arriving in Birmingham, his training began. Like most country people he could ride, but had to be re-taught how to ride in a military manner. His day began with a trumpet call at either a quarter to five, in the summer, or at six o'clock in the winter. Washing, dressing and folding bedding had to be done within fifteen minutes, after which the "stable" trumpet was sounded. The horses were mucked out and then exercised. A breakfast of coffee and bread was arranged either before or after training in the riding school, depending on the rota and the degree of training required. Horses were then fed and smartened up. Two hours of foot drill before lunch followed, the horses being fed this time before the men. After lunch more foot drill, sword exercises, or both, followed, until a short period of free time in the afternoon before six o'clock stables roll-call. Final rubbing-down and feeding for the horses finished the trooper's day, unless he had kit to clean, and most had. After that he was free either to lie on his bed or go into the town; no evening meal was provided by the Army.

Somerville's account of the passage through Parliament of the Reform Bill of 1831-32 is lucidly chronological and indicates clearly how the Army was affected by and implicated in most of the stages of its passage. No ordinary soldiers had the vote; most officers – by reason of their background and position – were opposed to Reform. The soldiers came from the same backgrounds as those classes pressing with increasing violence for improved Parliamentary representation, and yet they represented the power of the State. The Duke of Wellington, the most respected soldier in the Army and an absolute opponent of Reform, was influential in the House of Lords and was shortly to become the Prime Minister; his motives and intentions were

Pair of silver wine jugs. Presented to the Officers of the Royal Scots Greys by Colonel Arthur, Baron Sandys of Ombersley Court, County of Worcester, and their late Lt. Colonel, in token of his sincere regard for them, as well as to testify the pleasure he experienced during the many years he was associated with them and the pride he felt in having the command of that distinguished Regt. September 1839. *Decorated with the Sandys arms and the Regimental crest. Hallmark: London 1839-40. Maker: Benjamin Smith III*

A detachment of the Royal Scots Greys, with supply wagons, in an Irish village c. 1848. Watercolour in the manner of Michael Angelo Hayes.

persistently suspected by the radical element in Parliament and by the radical press. The Bill passed the Commons, eventually, in July 1831; it was rejected by the Lords in October 1831. The King prorogued Parliament on 20 October and warned that Reform would be reintroduced in the next session. The Bristol riots erupted on 29 October. As political unions were formed throughout industrial areas of Britain, so troops were placed in readiness to deal with the expected revolution; the Greys sharpened swords and had troops saddled, booted and spurred twenty-four hours a day. The Reformers were afraid of the power of the Army, whilst the establishment doubted the loyalty of the soldiers; a Revolution in France in 1830 had made the government even more jittery than usual. In April 1832 the Bill passed Commons and Lords but failed at the Committee stage. The strength and numbers of the political unions grew, and Somerville records two hundred thousand people attending a political meeting in Birmingham, five thousand of whom had, the week before, entered the barracks in a show of strength. The barracks were sealed off and orders issued for plans to stop the expected march by the Birmingham political union on London.

It was at this point, as a clash between the Greys and political protesters seemed inevitable, that Somerville and other troopers of the Regiment began to write letters to the press, to the King, to the Duke of Wellington, saying that they would not sabre peaceful citizens seeking to make a non-violent protest. It seems likely that they were not the only ones, and Somerville maintains that it was only once the establishment realised that the Army could no longer be relied upon to support them that the anti-Reformers gave way and allowed the passage of the Bill through the Committee stage in May 1832. That the doubtful reliability of the Army was one cause of the passage of the Bill was, not surprisingly, denied by the Duke of Wellington. His denial was quoted in the newspaper, the *Weekly Dispatch*. Reading the denial, towards the end of May 1832 while on guard but off duty, Somerville wrote a refutation of it. If his words can be believed, the motives of he and his comrades were never in doubt.

> The Scots Greys have honourably secured a high character in the defence of their country, and they would be the last to degrade themselves below the dignity of British soldiers, in acting as the tools of a tyrant.

Whatever his motives, it was clear that as far as the Regiment was concerned, Somerville had gone too far. Irrespective of his or his colleagues' rights, real or imaginary, there could have been no doubt that a thinly-concealed state of mutiny existed in the Greys. Although all the letters were anonymous, after various regimental investigations Somerville was accused of writing the letter which substantiated all the other letters, and he was brought before the senior major, Charles Wyndham, an officer who had been wounded in the foot at Waterloo. Wyndham was commanding the Greys in the absence on leave of the Lieutenant-Colonel, Lord Arthur Hill, and, while clearly perturbed that such a promising recruit as Somerville should have become involved in mutiny, he realised that an example had to be made in order to curb dissent. A court martial was hastily convened (too hastily, a Court of Enquiry subsequently decided) and, found guilty of a crime apparently unconnected with what Major Wyndham referred to as a "libel upon the Regiment", Somerville was sentenced to be flogged: two hundred lashes with the cat-o'-nine-tails. Somerville's account of his flogging is, not surprisingly, one of the few articulate accounts to survive. His elevation to the position of radical folk hero rapidly followed. The gossip in Birmingham about his flogging was fed by a characteristically lucid letter from Somerville which was published in Birmingham, London and Edinburgh newspapers, and "Somerville of the Greys" became as well-known a popular martyr as Ewart had been a popular hero. The Court of Enquiry – which the Horse Guards could not avoid, given the frenzied publicity – sat at Weedon in July 1832, having been forced to convene by a petition to the House of Commons. It became clear during the enquiry that Major Wyndham had wished to keep the matter as regiment-ally private as possible and had acted too rapidly in convening the court martial, passing sentence and implementing it. That he did what appeared to him to be the right thing for the right reasons was accepted, and Wyndham was merely repri-

Silver sugar caster. Presented in memory of Brevet Major James Reginald Tovin Graham, Cornet, Lieutenant and Captain, Royal Scots Greys, who served with them at Waterloo. *Hallmark: London 1772-73 Maker unidentified*

Two silver coffee pots:
Left: Presented to the Mess of the 3rd Dragoon Guards by Lieut. H. de C. Lawson 1850 *Hallmark: London 1849-50 Maker unidentified*
Right: Presented to the Officers' Mess Scots Greys by Captain Henry Sales Scobell on retiring from the Regiment 1856. *Hallmark: London 1854-55 Maker R and S Garrard and Co.*

manded. Somerville was allowed to purchase his discharge and went on to pursue a career in journalism. Wyndham commanded the Regiment from 1837 to 1841.

The year after the Somerville case the Greys were moved to York and then spent the years 1834 and 1835 in Scotland. In 1836 the Regiment was posted to Ireland, where it remained until 1843, returning there in 1846 after two years in England and Scotland. In 1851 the Greys returned to England and in 1853 took part in the "Camp of Exercise" on Chobham Common. This camp was the first real attempt to teach officers and men about the exigencies of active service, something which none of the Dragoon or Dragoon Guards regiments had experienced since the end of the Napoleonic Wars, nearly forty years before. The camp ran from June to August 1853 and the Greys were reviewed by Queen Victoria, who visited Chobham in August. Unfortunately for the troops who formed the vanguard of those sent to the Crimea in 1854, the numerous deficiencies which Chobham revealed in training and preparedness for the realities of war were exposed too late to be remedied before the onset of the real thing.

The Regiment was the last regiment of the Heavy Cavalry Brigade to leave England for the Crimea and the first to arrive, its speed being ensured by travel direct from Istanbul (Constantinople) to the Crimea, not via Bulgaria. Trumpeter Harry Powell of the 13th Light Dragoons recorded twenty years later in his reminiscences that the Greys landed looking as clean as if they were going to be reviewed in Hyde Park. The

The officers of the 3rd Dragoon Guards mounted for a review in the Phoenix Park, Dublin, 1852. The Regiment is formed up in the background to rank past by troop, with the band in front. The Commanding Officer, his trumpeter behind him, directs the officers to their positions. Watercolour. Artist: Michael Angelo Hayes

Battle of the Alma had been fought four days before the Greys set foot on Russian soil, on 20 September 1854, but it had not involved any of the light cavalry regiments who were already there. Victory at the Alma meant that the French and British Armies could advance on Sebastopol, and this is what happened. Once Sebastopol was besieged, a supply port near at hand was needed, so the port of Balaklava was captured. Once captured, its position on a line of communication was in jeopardy from a regrouped Russian force which had left Sebastopol before the siege in order not to be bottled up. The attempts by the Russians to retake Balaklava led to the battle on 25 October.

Few battles have inspired such evocative commemoration as that of Balaklava: the Thin Red Line, the Charge of the Light Brigade, the Charge of the Heavy Brigade. Essentially a cavalry action, for the good reason that the majority of the infantry were besieging Sebastopol, two hours' march away, Balaklava also involved horse artillery, the 93rd Highlanders and quantities of Turkish troops. As an immense Russian force gradually advanced towards Balaklava, pounding and then occupying the outlying redoubts, the cavalry retired before them, being covered by the light guns of the horse artillery. The principal actions took place on the floors of a series of wide valleys, each of which was interspersed by ridges and hills which blocked the view from the valley

Officer's cap, light troop, Royal Regiment of North British Dragoons c.1760.

Officer's helmet, 6th Dragoon Guards, pattern worn 1812 to 1818.

The Eagle of the 45th French Infantry, taken by Sergeant Charles Ewart of the 2nd (or Royal North British) Dragoons at the Battle of Waterloo, 18 June 1815.

Lieutenant General Sir Samuel Hawker KCH, 1835. Hawker, who became a General in 1838 and a Knight Grand Cross of the Royal Hanoverian Guelphic Order in 1836, was Colonel of the 3rd Dragoon Guards from 1831 until his death in 1838. In this picture he wears the uniform of a Lieutenant General and the Badge of a Knight (not Knight Commander) of the Royal Hanoverian Guelphic Order. He is attended by an orderly of the 3rd Dragoon Guards. Artist: James Pardon (fl. 1811-1848).

Lieutenant-Colonel Charles Wyndham with officers and other ranks of the Royal Scots Greys, and two officers of the Royal Horse Artillery, in the Phoenix Park, Dublin 1838. Wyndham, who had been a subaltern at the Battle of Waterloo, where he was wounded in the foot, is the dismounted figure in the right foreground, in full dress uniform. Artist: John Ferneley, Senior (1782-1860).

The Charge of the Heavy Brigade, 25th October 1854. The Greys are depicted hacking their way into the Russian cavalry, having been joined by the regimental butcher who can be seen slightly right of centre in the middle of the action. Artist: Félix Philippoteaux (1815-1884).

A troop of the 3rd Dragoon Guards in marching order, probably on exercise, c.1865. In the left foreground is the Troop Sergeant-Major. Watercolour. Artist: Orlando Norie (1832-1901).

The 6th Dragoon Guards, led by the Commanding Officer and his trumpeter, charging in line through the Long Valley near Aldershot, on manoeuvres c.1870. On the Regiment's right are the Royal Horse Artillery and, to their rear, another regiment of Dragoon Guards, possibly the 2nd (Bays). Watercolour. Artist: Orlando Norie (1832-1901).

Wine cistern of German silver, in the form of a man-of-war, or Nef, late nineteenth century. Presented to the Officers, Royal Scots Greys, from Major Crabbe, on leaving the Regiment 1902.

Major General Sir Nevill Smyth VC KCB (1868-1941) c.1923. General Smyth was commissioned into the 2nd Dragoon Guards (Queen's Bays) in 1888 and served in India and in the Sudan campaign of 1897-98, winning the Victoria Cross at the Battle of Khartoum in 1898. He transferred to the 6th Dragoon Guards in 1903, commanded the Carabiniers from 1909 until 1913 and was Colonel of the 3rd Dragoon Guards from 1920 until 1922 and Joint-Colonel of the combined Regiment from 1922 until 1925. He is depicted as Colonel of the 3rd/6th Dragoon Guards in service dress uniform with the neck Badge and Star of a Knight Commander of the Order of the Bath and the neck Badge of a Commander of the Belgian Order of Leopold. Artist: William McInnes (1889-1939).

Major General Henry Leader CB (1865-1934). General Leader joined the Carabiniers as a captain in 1897, after serving twelve years in the 2nd Bn. The Suffolk Regiment. He commanded the Regiment from 1905 until 1909 and is depicted here as the Commanding Officer, about 1909. He was made a Companion of the Order of the Bath in 1912, commanded the 1st Indian Cavalry Division between 1914 and 1917 and was Colonel of the Carabiniers from 1917 until 1922, and Joint-Colonel of the combined Regiment until 1925.
Artist unknown.

Field Marshal Sir William Robertson Bart. GCB GCMG GCVO DSO DCL LLD (1860-1933). Field Marshal Roberston served in the ranks of 16th (The Queen's) Lancers from 1877 until 1888, when he was commissioned into the 3rd Dragoon Guards, serving with the Regiment until 1892. He was awarded the DSO for the Chitral campaign of 1894. In 1915 he was appointed Chief of the Imperial General Staff and held the position until 1918. From 1916 until 1925 he was Colonel of the Royal Scots Greys, from 1925 until 1929 Colonel of the 3rd/6th Dragoon Guards and from 1929 until his death Colonel of The Royal Horse Guards (The Blues). He is depicted here in 1921 in the full dress uniform of a field marshal beneath the mantle of a Knight Grand Cross of the Order of the Bath.
Artist: John St. H. Lander (1869-1944).

The Tercentenary tank parade of The Royal Scots Dragoon
Guards, Princes Street, Edinburgh, 6 July 1978. Chieftain
Main Battle Tanks are depicted passing the saluting base, next
to the Royal Scots Greys South African War Memorial.
Taking the salute is HRH Prince Edward, Duke of Kent.
Artist: Ken Howard (1932-   )

The Officers' Mess dining room, Bhurtpore Barracks,
Tidworth, Hampshire 1988. Arranged on the dining table are
the silver goblets used in the Mess for port at the end of formal
dinners. Each has been given to the Mess by an officer on
leaving the Regiment, a tradition begun by Field Marshal Sir
John Stanier, who presented a pair of goblets on relinquishing
command of the Royal Scots Greys in 1968. On the far wall is
the Serov portrait of H.I.M. Tsar Nicholas II and in the
fireplace are a pair of framed music-stand covers of Queen
Victoria's reign.

A sentry of the Royal Scots Greys, in front of a rustic sentry-box, behind which are troopers of the Regiment cleaning their kit following a Royal review of the Regiment at the Camp of Exercise on Chobham Common, Surrey, August 1853. Watercolour in the manner of Henry Alken

Two farriers of the Royal Scots Greys shoeing a horse at the Regiment's mobile field forge while, in the background, troopers of the Regiment relax around a hastily-constructed bread-oven at the Camp of Exercise on Chobham Common, Surrey, August 1853. Watercolour in the manner of Henry Alken

floor. This visual impediment was not identified by the Generals, who saw the action from six hundred feet up, on the heights at one end of the valleys. Thus, as the five regiments of the Heavy Brigade advanced eastwards along the north side of the southern valley floor, they were unaware that advancing westwards above them, behind hills and ridges which separated the two parallel valleys, was a vastly superior mass of Russian cavalry. As the Heavy Brigade halted, so the Russians began, coincidentally it appears, to wheel left – neither side being aware of the other's existence. First sight of the opposing forces seem to have been of mutual surprise and a few moments were spent in manoeuvring for the inevitable clash.

The Russians extended their line to their left, the Heavies wheeled left into line, closed and dressed ranks and, uphill, charged. The Russians made no use of their superior position on a downward slope but received the charge motionless, having halted their downward advance to fire their carbines, a shot from one of which wounded the Greys' Commanding Officer, Lieutenant-Colonel Henry Darby Griffith. The Heavies' Commander, Brigadier The Hon. James Scarlett, led the front rank of the Brigade, formed of the Greys and 6th Inniskilling Dragoons, straight into the centre of the Russian horsemen, whose flanking squadrons extended to encircle the British. As the Russian pincer closed, so the 5th Dragoon Guards slammed into them on the Greys' left and the first squadron of the Inniskillings executed a similar manoeuvre on the right; the pincer had closed too soon. The remaining regiments of the Brigade, 4th Dragoon Guards and 1st Royal Dragoons, arrived after the mêlée was well under way and contributed to the gradual collapse and retreat of the Russian cavalry.

Rally the Greys! *A depiction, painted in 1895, of the incident during the Charge of the Heavy Brigade when the Greys, in danger of becoming dispersed in the mêlée, were rallied by the adjutant, Lieutenant William Miller – the bearded figure with sword held aloft in the centre of the picture. Presented to the Regiment by J K Stuart OBE, 1927. Artist: Allan Stewart (1865-1951)*

Once the two masses were joined there was little use of firearms. This was essentially a sword-to-sword engagement and, with the ineffective nature of the weapons used on both sides, actual deaths were few among the British, although horrific injuries were received. Cutting, chopping and slashing, the Greys milled about, each man fighting his own opponent, the shock effect of the charge dissipated but the advantage of height gradually beginning to tell (on average the Heavies were taller, when mounted, than their Russian adversaries). As the Russians faltered and fell back, so a troop of horse artillery came into action on their flank and, firing twenty-four-pound howitzer shells into them, completed the defeat.

Later on the morning of 25 October the Heavy Brigade was again ordered into action to cover the retreat of the shattered Light Brigade from its own charge and, this time, its casualties from musketry and artillery fire were considerable, the Greys suffering many more casualties than they had done earlier in the day.

Two Victoria Crosses were later awarded to men of the Greys who distinguished themselves at Balaklava – Sergeant Major James Grieve, for saving an officer's life, and Trooper Henry Ramage, for rescuing three of his comrades, two of whom were wounded and one of whom was a prisoner.

The cavalry were little used in the campaign after Balaklava and the appalling Crimean winter of 1854-55 finished off the carnage begun in those battles. The Greys returned home from the Crimea in July 1856 to another long period of peace.

CHAPTER FOUR

Foreign Adventures and Domestic Peace

1857-1880

3rd Dragoon Guards

In rather less than a year after the soldiers had returned from the Crimea in 1856, another panic galvanised the government into military action: the Indian Mutiny. Like most cataclysmic events, affecting large numbers of people and involving a potent mixture of religion, politics, personal ambition, money and racial tension, the causes of the Mutiny were far from simple and certainly not immediate or short-term.

Britain had assumed, through the East India Company, an increasing presence in India since the acquisition of Bombay by the Crown as part of the dowry of Catherine of Braganza, Queen to King Charles II, in 1661. For a long time this presence had been confined to trading possessions on the coast, and had been commercial and not political in nature. During the Seven Years War of 1756-63 the French had been virtually thrown out of the sub-continent by a combination of British and Indian Armies, and later campaigns in the 1780s and 1790s had firmly established Britain's military and political presence in India alongside her very lucrative commercial one. Small wars, sometimes of conquest but also of defence, continued during the first two decades of the nineteenth century, but serious territorial expansion did not begin until the 1840s, with the acquisition of a degree of hard-won influence in Afghanistan and the territories of Sind and the Punjab.

Britain was beginning to discover the first itch of the Imperial conscience: a

Two silver wine jugs.
Left: Presented to the Officers of the 3rd Prince of Wales Dragoon Guards by Lt J D Hay Hill on his leaving that corps, November 1853. *Hallmark: London 1849-50. Maker: John Samuel Hunt for Hunt and Roskell*
Right: Presented to the Officers' Mess, 3rd Prince of Wales' Dragoon Guards by Lieut. Norwood on promotion June 18th 1857. *Hallmark: London 1856-57. Maker: Edward Barnard and Sons*

belief that "we" knew better than "them" about managing things, and so the flavour of the Indian experience began to change, gradually but irreparably. No longer was there a close and friendly link between Briton and Indian in running Indian affairs for mutual benefit; rather – and imperceptibly at first – a "master and servant" relationship was allowed to develop. As the number of Christian missionaries increased, so did the number of civil administrators and, from the 1840s, the number of *memsahibs*. The glorious cocktail of cultures that was India began to feel threatened, hemmed in and in danger of suffocation by a crisply-starched blanket of Anglo-Saxon Christian disapproval.

For more than fifty years, prior to the outbreak of the Mutiny, the regiments of the East India Company's armies had been officered by Britons who had devoted their lives to their regiments and their men, learning their languages and studying their cultures. Gradually, in the last decade before the explosion of wrath that became the Mutiny, this changed. The new breeds of officer were no longer interested and tolerant; they were distant, arrogant and ignorant.

The annexation of the Kingdom of Oudh, whose ruler was senile and corrupt, in 1856 convinced many rulers of small independent Indian states that their turn would come; they were probably right. In the same year, the Governor-General announced that Indian troops would be liable for service overseas; for Hindus, to cross the sea involved losing caste. Evangelical Christianity was on the march too, with all its well-known discretion and subtlety, convincing Hindu and Moslem alike that their faith was under threat. Moslems dreamt of a reborn ruling Moslem dynasty with the restoration of the Moghuls.

Lastly, rumour, legend and superstition combined with tactical opportunity. It was rumoured that a new cartridge, greased with a tallow made from pig and cow fat, was to be compulsorily issued; pigs are unclean to Moslems, cows sacred to Hindus. A legend grew up that one hundred years after the Battle of Plassey

Silver tankard.
Presented to the Officers, 3rd (or PWLs) Dragoon Guards from Captain C B Melville on his retirement from the Regiment. *(1858). Hallmark: London 1868-69. Maker: Daniel and Charles Houle*

Two silver wine jugs.
Left: Presented by Colonel Custance *(6th D.G.)* to his brother officers July 1861. *Hallmark: London 1860-61. Maker: Henry Wilkinson and Co.*
Right: Presented to the Officers' Mess of the 3rd or Prince of Wales's Dragoon Guards by Sir Arundell Neave, Baronet, on his leaving the Regiment *(1863). Hallmark: London 1862-63. Maker: John Samuel Hunt for Hunt and Roskell*

(1757), when the French had been effectively driven from India, the British would follow them. British troops had appeared invincible in the eyes of many Indians; this superstition was seriously weakened by the reverses of the Crimean War – stories of which were spread in India, and exaggerated too, by Russian agents. The Crimean War had removed British troops from India and the number of Indian soldiers had had to be increased in consequence.

Indicative of the supreme insensitivity to Indian affairs which had developed gradually from the late 1830s is the fact that the outbreak of the Mutiny came as a complete shock to the British. Complacent in their paternal self-righteousness, they were first shocked, then hurt, then very, very angry. Suppression of the Mutiny became less of a military operation than a crusade against the forces of darkness and depravity, and the vigour of the troops in hunting out and dispatching mutineers was fuelled by frequently unquestioned, and often sadly true, horror stories of massacre, rape, torture and mutilation.

Britain's economic strength was closely linked to her possession of India. She could have afforded, except perhaps in terms of national prestige, to have lost the Crimean War; she could not afford to lose India. Consequently, reinforcements were rushed out by the quickest means to prop up forces in the presidencies of Bombay and Madras, which had not yet burst into flames as had Bengal. The 3rd Dragoon Guards sailed for India in August 1857, the Commanding Officer, Lieutenant-Colonel John Dyson, the Riding Master, Lieutenant William Blenkinsop, and four sergeants preceding them by the overland route in order to

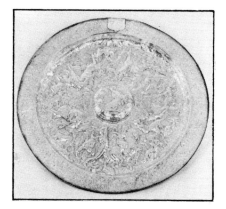

Embossed, silver-plated dish depicting scenes of classical warfare and decorated with classical motifs. Attached is a plaque of Sheffield silver (hallmark 1806-07) engraved: Presented by the Subalterns of the 9th Royal Lancers In Memory of the Picket Duty of 1867.

secure and train sufficient horses for the Regiment on its arrival. The Regiment, adequately mounted, was split up by troop or half-troop after arrival in Bombay, and was part of the Central India Field Force commanded by General Sir Hugh Rose, later Field Marshal Lord Strathnairn, which mopped up the few mutineers in central India and prevented large quantities of those fleeing from recriminations in the north, where the Mutiny had been centred, from gaining access to the asylum offered in the dominions of the Nizam of Hyderabad. By the end of the campaign it was based in Mhow with one wing at Ahmednagar.

The next decade was spent in the presidency of Bombay, which retained this designation despite the termination of the East India Company's rule in India, where the Regiment became acclimatised. Postings to India were, because of the length of travelling time and amount of trauma involved, frequently as long in the nineteenth century as postings are today for armoured regiments to Germany. Home leave was only rarely an option for the soldiers, but officers would receive furlough for several months every few years. In the years following the Mutiny it became apparent that India had changed and, while the Indian Army developed its own style to an extent unthought-of by the Company's regiments, the two communities of Britons and Indians remained irretrievably separate.

The second half of the nineteenth century was one of unmitigated Imperial expansion for Britain, one of new territories, wider still and wider possessions, of gunboat diplomacy and of a concentration on Imperial affairs to the almost total exclusion of those developing in Europe.

The campaign in Abyssinia (Ethiopia) in 1867 and 1868 was one of the few which did not involve the acquisition of new territories for Britain. More of a relief expedition than a campaign, its intention was to rescue European hostages held captive by the reportedly demented Emperor of Abyssinia, Theodore III. Negotiations with Theodore had been protracted, and increasingly difficult, since

Section of a silver drum, banded in silver-gilt, captured during the Abyssinian campaign 1867-68. Supported on an Abyssinian shield and mounted and embellished in English silver (hallmark London 1868-69) by Edward Barnard and Sons. The other two sections, the middle and other end, belong to two of the other British regiments whose predecessors fought in the campaign: The King's Own Royal Border Regiment and The Duke of Wellington's Regiment. The original drum was reputed to have been made for Queen Nelim of Abyssinia in 1440.

1864 and, eventually, the government in London decided that an armed expedition was the only answer. The troops most closely located to Abyssinia were those of the Bombay Army, commanded by Lieutenant-General Sir Robert Napier, a veteran of campaigns in India and China since 1845. Napier decided upon a landing on Abyssinia's Red Sea coast, followed by a march inland, and divided his available force into three brigades, placing the right wing of the 3rd Dragoon Guards in the third brigade, together with two Indian cavalry and five Indian infantry regiments and the 26th (Cameronians).

The third brigade had arrived in Abyssinia in March 1868, by which time Napier and the advance guard had penetrated more than 200 miles into the interior, towards the plateau fortress of Magdala where the hostages were held and the Abyssinian army massed. The Regiment took twenty-nine days to cover the 400 miles to Magdala and caught up with Napier and his storming forces as they were planning to attack the fortress. The right wing of the Regiment was formed of three troops, consisting of 204 officers and men, 224 horses and 257 Indian servants. Rapidity of movement and security of the lines of communication were essential. No one could ensure that the hostages would not be killed. The entire trek was through country with a hostile climate, and through the lands of Abyssinian princes whose degree of neutrality was only temporarily assured by bags of gold coins. Consequently, only 173 soldiers of the Regiment were at the storming of Magdala and only seventy-eight servants were retained.

The Regiment was armed for the campaign with the breech-loading Snider carbine, a single-shot weapon firing a large-calibre lead bullet from a brass cartridge. The Snider was a new weapon and the Regiment was one of the first to be armed with it. Campaigning dress was employed too: loose linen blouses and trousers replaced the scarlet tunic and blue overalls and cork sun helmets replaced their brass equivalents. The value of a type of service dress had been recognised as early as the late 1840s in India and had been widely used, in a variety of non-uniform styles, during the Indian Mutiny. It would become increasingly employed as campaigns in hot climates continued and its colour, khaki (from the Persian word for dust or earth) would become as inextricably associated with the British soldier as scarlet had once been.

The Abyssinian climate was far from ideal for any sort of campaigning by European troops and was especially bad for horses. The cavalry was principally used to secure perimeters and to seal off potential escape routes from Magdala. On the route back the spring rains began and turned a dust-bowl into a mud-bath; forty-five horses and two soldiers died before the Regiment left for England at the end of May. The remaining three troops, which formed the left wing, quitted Bombay a day later, and the two wings were united with the Depot in Chichester in November 1868.

Among the many trophies removed as part of the "spoils of war" from Magdala was a silver drum reputedly dating from the fifteenth century. Napier ordered that it should be divided between three of the British regiments present at the fall of the fortress, and so the Regiment acquired one of its most permanent battle trophies, which it had further embellished by a London silversmith and mounted upon an Abyssinian shield. The other two sections of the drum remain with the King's Own Royal Border Regiment – successors of the 4th Foot, and the Duke of Wellington's Regiment – successors of the 33rd Foot.

The 3rd Dragoon Guards remained in southern England for the next seven years until being posted to Ireland in 1875. England had quietened down a lot since the days of Chartism and Reform, but Ireland was gradually moving towards unified and articulate concepts of Home Rule, and the manifestations of these were to keep British soldiers in Ireland actively engaged in attempting to keep the peace throughout the island for the next fifty years. The Regiment remained in Ireland until 1882.

Silver table centrepiece.
A memorial to the officers and men of the 6th Dragoon Guards
killed during the Crimean War and Indian Mutiny. Hallmark:
London 1861-62. Maker: R and S Garrard and Co.

6th Dragoon Guards

The Carabiniers landed in India at Chinsura, now in the northern suburbs of Calcutta, in December 1856. Chinsura was the northernmost deepwater anchorage on the River Hooghly, and most British regiments disembarking for service in the Bengal Presidency of the East India Company's territories landed there. From Chinsura the Regiment was embarked upon barges up the Hooghly to the Ganges and towed along the Ganges to Allahabad. From Allahabad, after making camp for a short period, the Carabiniers marched along the Grand Trunk Road to Meerut, a major British military cantonment forty miles north-east of Delhi, which was reached on 18 March 1857.

On arrival in Meerut they received their horses, 621 in all. Half of them were from government stud farms and the remainder were the cast-offs of Indian cavalry regiments. By being posted to India the Regiment had had to increase its establishment by well over one hundred per cent (the Indian regimental establishment being 790 soldiers of all ranks). In consequence a large number of recruits were untrained and fully half the horses either unbroken or unbreakable. The Regiment's nominal strength was 652; its effective strength would have been about half that. All the British regiments in Meerut were under-strength and totalled, at most and nominally, 1,700 men. Cantoned with them were three regiments of the Bengal Army, totalling 2,230 white officers and Indian other ranks. Unluckily for the Carabiniers, the Indian Mutiny began in Meerut.

The issue of the greased cartridges, which was only the catalyst for the Mutiny, came to a head in Meerut on 23 April when the 3rd Bengal Light Cavalry refused, on parade, to handle them. An example was made, eighty-five *sowars* (troopers) being court-martialled and sentenced to ten years' hard labour. The Carabiniers were detailed to provide an escort for the prisoners, whose harsh sentences seemed to their comrades disproportionately severe, given their defence of acting to preserve their faith.

The Indian regiments in Meerut seethed with mounting indignation for a fortnight, during which time opportunities were taken to establish the degree of support that a co-ordinated rising might attract from Indian regiments cantoned elsewhere in Bengal. On 10 May *sepoys* (privates) of the 11th and 20th Bengal Native Infantry, together with a mob from the bazaar, began a riot, killed some of their officers and induced the 3rd Light Cavalry to join them. The gaol was broken open, buildings set alight and several more Europeans were murdered. The Carabiniers' lines were closest to those of the Indian regiments and, as news of the uprising spread, the Regiment mounted all the men that it could and assembled with the other British regiments, ready for action. By the time that all the British troops were prepared, all the rolls called and some sort of appraisal made of the situation, darkness had fallen and the movements of the mutineers were unknown.

In fact they were marching on Delhi and reached there without being prevented. Delhi was occupied, its Indian regiments joined the Mutiny and British power in the city was eradicated. A troop of the Carabiniers rode down and sabred a party of Bengal Sappers and Miners on the road from Meerut to Delhi on 16 May. Two squadrons of the Regiment formed part of the force which left Meerut to lay siege to Delhi at the end of the month. At Ghazi-ud-din Nagar on 30 May, this small force was attacked by some 5,000 mutineers who had left Delhi for the purpose. The Carabiniers supported the artillery, who silenced the mutineers' guns and added to the slaughter executed by the 60th Rifles, the Carabiniers' squadrons under Lieutenant-Colonel William Custance and Captain Charles Rosser pursuing the fleeing mutineers for several miles after the battle. The mutineers tried again the following day, with similar results, and in the two

Silver inkstand.
Presented to the Officers of the Carabiniers by Captain
Bruce, Carabiniers 1862. Hallmarks indistinct. Maker:
Elkington, Mason and Co.

Pair of silver ice pails.
Presented to his brother officers by Major Bott on
his retirement from the Regiment *(6th D.G.)* in
which he had served 13 happy years, April 1864.
Hallmark: London 1863-64. Maker: Crespel and
Parker

actions the Regiment lost six killed and eight wounded.

At Alipur on 7 June the small Meerut force was joined by two brigades coming
south from Ambala, to form a siege train of about 3,500 men, plus perhaps 20
times as many Indian servants. The 9th Lancers, who had been in India since 1842,
contrasted comfortably in their white hot-weather uniforms with the
Carabiniers' two squadrons who were still clad in heavy blue tunics and overalls.
The two regiments formed the British regular cavalry part of the cavalry brigade
under the leadership of Brigadier James Hope Grant, one of the most expert
cavalry soldiers of his time.

The Carabiniers squadron commanded by Colonel Custance led the division's
advance on Delhi on 8 June and attacked a force of mutineers entrenched at
Badli-ke-Serai, six miles outside the city. After a brief artillery duel the 75th
Regiment and 60th Rifles attacked with the bayonet, overran the mutineers'
positions and, aided by the 9th Lancers, captured eleven guns. The Carabiniers
were active in the pursuit and mopping-up operations as the division continued its
advance on Delhi.

The siege of Delhi was concentrated on the Ridge, a spur of land rising above
the city to the north and west which commanded the vital lines of communication
between Delhi and the Punjab. This siege lasted three months, and during that
period, throughout the summer heat and the monsoon. the Regiment's strength
was gradually reduced to one squadron, more by disease than from wounds.
Small actions were fought and,.at one, an under-strength troop of Carabiniers
recruits, commanded by Lieutenant James Stillman, was taken by surprise by a
body of mutineer cavalry and routed, their confusion being alleviated by prompt

action on the part of a horse artillery troop which came rapidly into action and dispersed the mutineers. Delhi was finally taken by storm in September and the Regiment detached to form part of a column which raided mutineer territories west of Delhi.

The two squadrons of the Regiment which marched from Meerut to Delhi and took part in the siege and capture were chiefly formed of seasoned soldiers and the better trained of the new recruits. Left behind in Meerut was the remainder of the Regiment, the left wing under Colonel Henry Jones, the Commanding Officer, which constituted much of the garrison of the city and spent several months in perfecting its training. Small expeditions were necessary against foraging bands of mutineers and, by July, the Carabiniers were able to mount another squadron of two troops which, commanded by Captain George Wardlaw, was in action several times between July and December 1857. At Narnul, in November, Wardlaw's squadron, together with one of the Guides' Cavalry, defeated the mutineer Jodhpur Legion in a spectacular cavalry charge against cavalry and guns. Attempting to repeat the experience a month later, across land intersected with *nullahs* (dry watercourses), Wardlaw and his two Lieutenants, John Hudson and Sydney Vyse, were killed when their chargers carried them further and faster towards a party of mutineers at Gangari than their supporting troopers were able to manage on their troop horses.

Early in 1858, with Delhi once again secure, a number of field forces and columns were formed for the express purpose of hunting down parties of mutineers which were still in the field in some force. Colonel Jones led a four-troop squadron of the Regiment as part of one of these columns, and was in action at the end of April at Kukrauli together with Cureton's Multani Horse. The two regiments repeatedly charged mutineers to clear the village. After Kukrauli, at which the force commander had been killed, command of the column devolved upon Colonel Jones, and he gave command of his squadron to Captain John Forster. Forster's squadron, with the rest of the force, marched towards a mutineer stronghold at Bareilly, where it was joined by part of the Roorkhi Field Force, which included a further Carabinier squadron under Captain Thomas Bott. After the successful assault on Bareilly a further squadron of the Carabiniers, commanded by Major Robert Bickerstaff, marched together with other regiments to the relief of the 82nd Foot, besieged in Shahjehanpur.

Between June and September 1858, whilst most active campaigning was halted because of the onset of the monsoon, the Regiment was split between Meerut, Moradabad and Shahjehanpur, its strength being computed at 748 officers and men and 703 horses. Campaigning began in November 1858 and two squadrons, the right wing of the Regiment under Colonel Jones, were assigned as escort to the

3 silver cups.
Left: Challenge Cup, the Smith Cup. Presented to Colonel Sawyer and the officers of the Carabiniers by Captn. Arthur George Smith on his leaving the Regiment, May 1866. *Hallmark: London 1866-67. Maker: Hunt and Roskell*
Centre: Welter Cup, the Burnley Cup. Presented by Captain H Burnley to the Carabiniers on promotion, December 15th 1869. *Hallmark: Edinburgh 1869-70. Maker: Michael Creighton and Co.*
Right: Regimental Challenge Cup, the Dakin Cup. Presented by Lt. W.E. Dakin to his brother officers on leaving the Regiment *(6th D.G.),* July 1863. *Hallmark: London 1863-64. Maker: R and S Garrard and Co.*

Pair of silver kettledrums.
Presented to Colonel Napier, the Officers and Men of the Carabiniers from Frederick Carne Rasch, Lieut.. In Memory of the 9 Years he had the honour to serve in the Regiment 1876. *Hallmark: London 1876-77. Maker: Henry Potter and Co.*

Commander-in-Chief, Lord Clyde. Clyde, who was at that time sixty-four years old, was the son of a Glasgow carpenter and had been a soldier since 1807. Rarely out of action, he had commanded the Highland Brigade at Balaklava, where he had made a point of congratulating the Greys on their part in the Charge of the Heavy Brigade. Noted for his terse Caledonian wit, he was far from colourful but desperately efficient and methodical as a soldier, possessed of the ideal dogged, determined qualities necessary for the long, slow business of suppressing the Mutiny. His campaign in Oudh in 1858 and 1859 effectively finished the Mutiny in northern India. The right wing returned to Muttra after the clearing of Oudh and was joined there in May 1859 by the left wing which, commanded by Colonel Custance, had been operating separately, first in the north of Oudh and then from Agra as part of the pursuit of Tantia Tope, the last uncaptured and unexecuted mutineer leader.

In the two years that the Carabiniers were engaged in the suppression of the Indian Mutiny, from May 1857 to May 1859, their casualties were 124 of all ranks. In return for this sacrifice, the battle honour "Delhi" was added to their standard.

After detaching a two-troop squadron as escort to the Viceroy between December 1859 and January 1860, the Carabiniers returned to peacetime soldiering in India for a brief spell before disembarking for Britain in January 1861. 134 volunteers were left behind, to join other cavalry regiments in India, and the Regiment landed at Gravesend in July 1861. Several of the officers, including Colonels Custance and Jones, had returned by the quicker, if personally more expensive, overland route. Colonel Jones had busied himself on his arrival in buying horses for the Regiment to be ready when it returned to Chatham. Regimental strength, when the Carabiniers landed, was 635 of all ranks but a third of the officers were shortly placed on half-pay and 180 of the soldiers demobilised to reduce the Regiment to its home establishment level.

Until 1865 the Carabiniers were stationed in south-east England, but in that year they were posted in great haste to Ireland for seven years to form part of the forces concentrated to attempt to deal with the Fenian troubles. The Fenians, or Fenian Brotherhood, a secret society originally organised in America in 1858, had as their principal aim the overthrow of British government in Ireland. Masterminded by exiled Irishmen who had been implicated in an abortive rising in 1848, it presented little real threat to peace in Ireland until after the end of the War between the States in 1865, when demobilised American officers of Irish extraction were encouraged to participate in an armed expedition to Ireland. Acting with the aid of informers, and suspending the Habeas Corpus Act, the government in Dublin swiftly rounded up most of the ringleaders and the presence of an increased military force in Ireland prevented any major disturbances. Fenian troubles continued in Canada though, and were transferred in the form of bombings and murders to the British mainland during the 1870s and 1880s.

Prior to their move to Ireland in 1865 the Carabiniers were presented with a pair of kettledrums by Cornet Hardin Burnley. Eleven years later, in 1876, after they had been at home for four years, the Regiment received another pair, in silver, from Lieutenant Frederic Carne Rasch, upon his retirement. Quite why the Carabiniers should have required a second set after only nine years is not recorded, although thoughts of an over-boisterous mess night do come to mind, but Rasch was handsomely thanked by the Commanding Officer in Regimental Orders for his generosity. Rasch subsequently became a Justice of the Peace, Deputy Lieutenant of Essex, Member of Parliament for south-east Essex from 1886 to 1900 and for mid-Essex from 1900 to 1908, and a baronet; his eldest son joined the Regiment from 1st Battalion The Essex Regiment in 1903.

In 1877 the Carabiniers embarked for India again and remained stationed at Amballa until the outbreak of the Second Afghan War in 1879. Orders were received to proceed to Afghanistan at the beginning of September 1879, and the entire Regiment was moved north to Jhelum at the end of the month by troop

Presentation sword.
Regimental pattern bowl hilt of the 6th Dragoon Guards.
Blade inscribed: From Colonel Napier to Major Fryer,
Dublin 1872, Officers' Prize for Swordsmanship.
Supplied by Henry Wilkinson and Co.

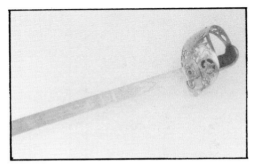

Pair of silver punchbowls.
Presented to the Officers' Mess, Carabiniers, by
Major Cadman on leaving the Regiment 1875.
*Hallmark: London 1874-75. Maker: F B Thomas
and Co.*

train. Delayed by a variety of differing orders, the Carabiniers eventually arrived
at the fortress of Jalalabad, via the Khyber Pass, in November, and were then
employed on patrols, escort duty and the protection of lines of communication.
Kabul, the capital, was occupied and its Amir, Yakub Khan, was captured and
exiled to India, under Carabiniers escort for part of the way. The British forces
defeated the Afghans at Charasiah and were themselves humiliated at Maiwand.
News of Maiwand, where the 66th Regiment had been massacred, induced
further Afghan uprisings, and a squadron of the Regiment was in action at Dakka
in January 1880 against some Mohmand tribesmen. Two moveable columns were
set up and these, together with forming part of the Jalalabad garrison, occupied
the Regiment's activities between March and July 1880. In July 1880 Captain
Henry Hamilton, commanding two troops, was part of a force sent to pacify
some Mohmand villages and, although operating his force over very unsuitable
terrain, encircled the Pathans and induced them, uncharacteristically, to
surrender. The relief of Kandahar at the end of the year ended the war, the
Carabiniers coming out of it with another battle honour and total casualties of
thirty-four other ranks. For the next five years the Carabiniers were based at
Sialkot, in the foothills of the western Himalayas.

Royal Scots Greys

On their return from the Crimea in 1856 the Greys were not posted abroad again
as a Regiment for forty-four years. The only other regiment to equal this record

Silver cup, the VC cup. Presented to the Officers' Mess, Royal Scots Greys, by George Cleghorn of Weens, Roxburghshire, late a Captain in the Regt. 1866. Mounted in relief on the bowl, which is a later addition to an earlier base, are the reverses of the Waterloo Medal 1815, Crimean War Medal 1854-56, Turkish Crimean War Medal 1854-56 and Long Service and Good Conduct Medal (Army) and the obverses of the Distinguished Conduct Medal and Sardinian Medal for Military Valour. Engraved beneath these are depictions of the Victoria Cross and the French Médaille Militaire. Hallmark (base): Edinburgh 1790 Maker: William Davie

was 1st The Royal Dragoons; even the Household Cavalry went abroad, to Egypt, between 1882 and 1885. Similarly to the Household Cavalry, the Greys sent a detachment to Egypt, but not until 1884, and so its achievements cannot be related in this chapter.

The Greys went to Ireland in 1857 and remained there until 1861. The next two years were spent in Scotland and the following two in England, before the Regiment returned to Ireland in 1866 to assist the strengthened garrison during the Fenian emergency. In 1872 they returned to Edinburgh and were posted to England in 1874, remaining there until 1878 before returning to Ireland for another four-year tour of duty in 1879.

Although little of regimental interest occurred, or is recorded, between 1857 and 1880, these twenty-three years were a period of considerable change within the Army as a whole and, naturally, some of these changes affected the cavalry. The Army which returned from the Crimean War had learnt a number of unpleasant lessons, the hard way, and it is to the credit of the Army's administration that, gradually, it chose to learn from its mistakes. In many ways the Army which went to the Crimea was little different, in equipment, attitudes or professionalism, to that which had fought Napoleon forty years before. While this may seem reprehensible, it must be remarked that the Allies' opponents in the Crimea were in much the same moribund state. Even the French Army, frequently held up as an example to the British, had changed very little in the preceding forty years.

Silver cup, The Royal Scots Dragoon Guards Inter-Squadron Athletics Cup. Presented from the Non-Commissioned Officers of the "Greys" to the Non-Commissioned Officers of the "Carabiniers", Aldershot 1873. Hallmark: London 1873-74. Maker: Alexander Macrae for Macrae and Goldstein.

Silver sugar bowls, with gilded interiors, in the form of kettledrums.
Pair: Presented to his brother officers *(6th D.G.)* by J. Moore, July 5th 1871. *Hallmark: London 1871-72. Maker: Edward Barnard and Sons*
Single: Presented to the Sergeants' Mess, Royal Scots Greys, by Colonel George Calvert Clarke 1866. *Hallmark: London 1866-67. Maker: Hunt and Roskell*

Most noticeable were the changes made to the soldiers' uniforms during and following the Crimean War. The Army all went to war in tight-fitting clothing admirably suited to an immaculate parade-ground appearance but quite unsuitable for fighting in. As has frequently happened, wartime conditions served to modify appearance very rapidly and, as photographs from the Crimea show, little remained of a parade-ground appearance by the winter of 1854. So looser, even baggy, uniforms were introduced by 1857 and, although the Greys retained their unique cavalry bearskin cap, they adopted a tunic rather than continuing with the old short-tailed coatee. Not until the end of the period under consideration here, or even well into the 1880s, would much consideration be given to the use of any form of uniform campaigning, or service, dress and, while such clothing might be issued for service overseas, its wear at home was unthinkable.

Weapons improved too. Cavalry soldiers, other than lancers, were taught until well into the 1860s that their principal weapon was the sword. The carbine was for use only in emergencies and, until the advent of a breech-loading weapon in 1864, was more trouble than it was worth to use while mounted. The reasons for the difficulty are easily understood if one considers that the carbine before 1864 was loaded via the muzzle. This operation necessitated tearing the bullet out of its paper cartridge (usually with the teeth), emptying the powder charge from the cartridge down the barrel, putting the remaining paper on top of it to form a wad, ramming that home and then ramming home the bullet last of all. Following those procedures, a tiny percussion cap, shaped like a minute thimble (and both fragile and unstable) had to be placed on the breech nipple, beneath the hammer. Not a difficult operation if dismounted, sheltered, dry, alert and not being shot at; almost impossible if mounted on a curvetting troop horse in the rain.

Under the circumstances it was not unreasonable for most commanding officers to concentrate on the sword until the arrival of a breech-loading carbine with a self-contained cartridge. The swords were far from ideal. Until, in theory, 1853 (but probably, in practice, several years later), light and heavy cavalry were issued with different swords. Initially, when the light cavalry concept had been created, their swords were curved and designed solely to cut. And cut they did, exceptionally well if kept sharp and properly handled. In view of the supposed role of the heavy cavalry, in restricting itself to the charge, their swords were designed principally to thrust, although the type used by Ewart and his comrades at Waterloo was far more effective when used as a cleaver. It also proved quite impossible to train troopers principally to thrust since, in a mêlée, and even the best charges ended in mêlées, the natural instinct was to cut and generally thrash about in the hope of connecting with something. The Commanding Officer of the Greys commented after Balaklava on the inferior nature of his men's swords when used in the cut against the Russians' thick greatcoats; only when used in a downward stroke against the head were they at all effective. Darby Griffith had also noted that the Russians' greatcoats had turned the points of his men's swords and there were several recorded instances of swords buckling under the thrust. Essentially, the problem was that the Heavies' swords were compromise weapons intended to be adequate for both cut and thrust and, of course, were not good at either manoeuvre. Even officers' swords were of better use for parade purposes than fighting and, as soon as this was realised, a great many officers had top-quality fighting swords made for the Crimea, as well as equipping themselves with one or two of the new revolving pistols; the men did not have this option.

A matter which affected the entire Army, with the exception of the Artillery and Engineers, was the ending of the purchase of commissions in 1871. All commissioned ranks up to and including regimental command could be purchased, and this system had been in operation since the creation of the standing Army in the middle of the seventeenth century. Although a system of prices had obtained, in theory, these operated frequently as little more than guides, and before 1860 cavalry commissions had always cost more than those in infantry regiments. Prior to 1860 the "advertised" price of a cornet's commission in the cavalry was £850, a lieutenant's £1,190, a captain's £3,225 and a major's £4,575. After 1860 these prices all dropped by between one-third and one-quarter. By the post-Crimea period, too, rules had been introduced to ensure that an officer spent some time in each rank before being allowed to purchase his promotion. The ending of the system cost the Government an estimated eight million pounds in compensation but began, gradually, the process of increased professionalism among commissioned ranks. The last officer of the Greys to purchase his commission was Cornet Montague Johnstone, on 22 June 1870, and the first officer to join after the abolition was Sub-Lieutenant William Firmstone, the rank of cornet having been given notice to quit at the same time as the abolition of purchase. Johnstone retired as a major, Firmstone as a lieutenant.

The Crimean War had other, longer-lasting, effects too. As a result of the absence of the regular regiments of the Army from Britain for, first the Crimea and then the Mutiny and the wars for Empire, auxiliary regiments were formed during the 1850s. The Yeomanry, which had been in a state of suspended animation since the days of civil unrest in the 1830s, was re-established in the 1850s. Scotland had five regiments of Yeomanry in 1860, most of which had adjutants who had seen service in a regular cavalry regiment. By 1880 the number had dropped to four regiments, all of whose adjutants were attached from regular regiments; the adjutant of the East Lothian Yeomanry being Captain Patrick Sanderson of the Greys. It did not follow, however, that Greys officers only served as adjutants in Scottish Yeomanry regiments and, also in 1880, Captain Edward Donnithorne was attached as adjutant to the Hertfordshire Yeomanry. This increased linking between regular regiments and their auxiliary comrades made for greatly increased efficiency among the latter and was part of a general rationalisation that had its most far-reaching effects among the infantry regiments under the reorganisation of 1881.

In 1866 the Regiment's soubriquet was finally officially acknowledged and, from being 2nd (Royal North British) Dragoons, the Regiment became 2nd (Royal North British) Dragoons (Scots Greys). In 1877 the title changed again to 2nd Dragoons (Royal Scots Greys). How long the soubriquet had been in use is not actually recorded, but its earliest use seems to have been in 1704 or 1705.

Silver statuette.
Presented by Captain John Smiley to the Officers of the Carabiniers in commemoration of the South African
War 1899-1902. *Hallmark: London 1904-05. Maker: Goldsmiths' and Silversmiths' Company Ltd*

CHAPTER 5

Marching Over Africa

1881-1902

3rd Dragoon Guards

Returning from Ireland in 1882, little the worse for their experiences in an island that was coming slowly to boiling point, the 3rd Dragoon Guards were posted to Scotland for a year. One hundred officers and men were detached as volunteers to join the 4th (Royal Irish) Dragoon Guards and 7th (Princess Royal's) Dragoon Guards for the campaign in Egypt in 1882.

Campaigning in Egypt and the Sudan was to occupy the British Army intermittently from 1882 until the end of the century, with renewed spasmodic involvement in that part of Africa until the Suez affair of 1956. As in that last swipe of the lion's paw, the conflict in 1882 involved influence around and upon the Suez Canal, rather newer in 1882 than seventy-four years later. The parallels, superficially at least, are remarkable. Britain and France were propping up a decadent régime, that of the Khedive Tewfik, which served their joint interests while not necessitating their active involvement, other than the occasional loan. Nationalist resentment, against the Khedive, who was a kind of Viceroy for the Sultan of Turkey, and against British and French exploitation of Egyptian resources, was orchestrated by Colonel Ahmed Arabi Bey, who stuck his neck out so persistently that, with great reluctance, the British Government decided upon sending an expeditionary force to sort him out. The French, after due consideration, decided not to become involved, and so all the fighting devolved upon Britain. Maintenance, both of supply lines and of fresh water resources, was all-important, and so the Suez Canal and its sweetwater canal were early targets for acquisition. Oddly, Arabi Bey did not either destroy or damage the Canal at the first appearance of British troops, and so the initial campaigning was aimed at securing viable strongpoints upon and around it. An important lock at Kassassin was secured by a troop of 4th Dragoon Guards on 26 August 1882 and, gradually, the rest of a small detachment reinforced Kassassin. Eventually the Egyptians decided that they should dislodge these soldiers, and advanced in strength to do so, extending their line of infantry to overlap the small British force. Reinforcements were summoned by heliograph and arrived after dark to execute the famous "moonlight charge" of the Household Cavalry, supported by 7th Dragoon Guards, which completely routed the Egyptians. Attached to the 7th Dragoon Guards was Lieutenant Henry Gribble, of the 3rd Dragoon Guards, who was also orderly officer to Colonel Sir Baker Russell. Russell commanded the 1st Brigade of the Cavalry Division and had been a Carabinier between 1855 and 1862. Gribble, apparently, had landed himself with an ungovernable charger which had a propensity to run away with its rider, usually in the wrong direction. Gribble was the only officer killed in the Kassassin charge, and his death is thought to have been due to the excitability of his mount.

The Egyptian campaign eventually accounted for another officer with 3rd Dragoon Guards associations. Major General Sir Herbert Stewart, Brigade Major in the Tel-el-Kebir campaign of 1882, and Commander of the Desert Column (which included some Greys) in the Sudan in 1884, had transferred to the 3rd in 1873 from the 37th (North Hampshire) Regiment at the age of thirty. In 1877 he attended the Staff College, a rare interest for a cavalry officer, and was admitted as a student to the Inner Temple, an achievement rare to the point of uniqueness for a cavalry officer. He became Military Secretary to Sir Garnet Wolseley in South Africa in 1880 and, had he not died from wounds on the relief expedition to save General Gordon in Khartoum in 1885, would undoubtedly have become a very distinguished general officer.

Stewart's adopted regiment received another who was destined for greatness in 1888. Second Lieutenant William Robertson joined the Regiment in that year in Mathura, on the River Jumna between Agra and Delhi, where it had been stationed since arriving in India in 1883. Robertson had been commissioned from the ranks of the 16th (The Queen's) Lancers, in which he had served since 1877, working his way from trooper to regimental sergeant-major in only eleven years. It was not unknown for soldiers to be commissioned in the nineteenth century, and was perhaps rather more common than has heretofore been believed; a successful and young regimental sergeant-major could often be commissioned, but rarely rose much beyond captain in rank. In addition to the talented and ambitious soldier who came from a poor background, the cavalry is known to

A trooper of the 3rd Dragoon Guards in marching order, with a group of country people, perhaps while on manoeuvres c. 1882. Watercolour. Artist: Orlando Norie (1832-1901)

have attracted recruits whose social status was demonstrably higher than the run-of-the-mill recruit in the infantry. Robertson was not among these, although his education put him on a par with sons of the middle class, but he seems to have had a dour determination to succeed. With no private income, he found the standards of the 3rd's officers' mess difficult to attain and, to his credit, did not attempt to compete. He remained with the Regiment as a regimental officer until 1892, attended the Staff College and rose steadily in rank until becoming Chief of the General Staff in 1915 and a principal architect of the victory of 1918. Retiring as a Field Marshal and a Baronet, "Wully" Robertson was Colonel of the Greys from 1916 until 1925 and of the 3rd Carabiniers from 1925 until 1929. It is tempting to imagine that these four years of his long and eventful life may have been the most rewarding, as Colonel of the Regiment which received him so hospitably forty years before.

The 3rd Dragoon Guards remained in India until 1892, playing polo, pig-sticking and enjoying all the benefits that post-Mutiny India offered. Servants were more than plentiful for all ranks, pay was higher and the amount of daily training possible was restricted to that capable of being carried out in the early morning when the weather was coolest. The forms of active recreation most associated with cavalry regiments were principally enjoyed by officers since a measure of extra income was necessary to afford polo and pig-sticking ponies; these activities also rapidly assumed social implications which made it difficult for interested soldiers to participate. Polo was a relatively new game to the British, being reintroduced to India in 1863, but it quickly caught on, and the first inter-regimental game in Britain was played in 1870. A local newspaper, reporting the game as "Hockey on Horseback", opined that the game was admirably suited to the cavalry and evinced an interest in the remarkably expressive language used by the players. If plentiful servants allowed the officers to indulge in recreation, they also encouraged lethargy and concomitant problems of alcoholism among officers and other ranks alike. In the heat of the day during the hot season there was little escape from either boredom or excessive warmth; thirst was constant and slaking it easy. Most regiments posted to India rapidly founded a branch of the Army Temperance Association and established recreation rooms and cricket teams to provide alternatives to spending the days horizontal on a bunk with a bottle.

In 1892 the 3rd Dragoon Guards left India for Natal and were stationed in Pietermaritzburg for three years before returning to England in 1895. While in South Africa, Captain Andrew Nolan and two non-commissioned officers served on detached duty with the Bechuanaland Police during the Matabele Rising of 1893. The Regiment was stationed in south-east England until 1898, when it moved to York for a year and thence to Ireland in 1899. The Home Rule campaign that was to convulse Ireland for the next two decades was well under way, with the various factions translating political discussion into street violence, and the 3rd remained in Ireland until January 1901, when the campaign in South Africa – which had seemed to be over – demanded their services.

The outbreak of the second Boer War occurred in 1899 and, as a result of the emergency, the Regiment's establishment was increased to 696 of all ranks, with 465 horses. Throughout the next year or so, drafts of men were sent to South Africa to serve in other units and, in March 1900, the establishment was further increased to 883 of all ranks.

The second stage of the war, after all the major battles had been fought and all the sieges relieved, was really a monumental mopping-up operation. The prospect was daunting since it was conducted across hundreds of thousands of square miles of veldt, against an enemy whose familiarity with the terrain, the climate and the last word in weapons technology made him not only formidable but also a more serious proposition than anything the British Army had had to face for more than

Silver cup. Highland Societies' Sports, 1st Prize – individual tent pegging, won by Sergt. W. Cousins, 3rd Dn. Gds., Cape Town, *6.10.02. Unhallmarked*

Pair of silver-plated statuettes, depicting soldiers of the Camel Corps 1884-1885. Presented by "Johnnie" Anderson to the Sergts. Mess "Scots Greys" May 1885.

forty years. It was a war which lent itself to cavalry operations, speed of movement and versatility being essential. The Boer commandos, mounted on small swift ponies, able to live on the parsimonious contents of their saddlebags, and frighteningly expert shots, caused Britain's cavalry soldiers to relearn the art of war. The British regular cavalry were accompanied by quickly-raised units of mounted infantry, by companies of imperial yeomanry, by Indian cavalry and by Australian light horse regiments, whose familiarity with similar terrain and conditions made them a valuable, if occasionally undisciplined, asset.

On arrival in South Africa the 3rd Dragoon Guards joined a column commanded by Colonel Edward Bethune of the 16th Lancers, which spent some time in pursuit of the Boer general Christian de Wet and his forces. The function of Bethune's force, allied with that of similar forces, was gradually to push the Boers back into a space with a guardable perimeter, behind the line of block houses and barbed wire which was being constructed to deny them access to supply routes, and so starve them into surrender. Rounding up Boer commandos was a little like trying to comb water into a pile, or eat soup with a fork, and the column was fairly constantly on the march and regularly in contact with the enemy. Raids by small mobile forces were found to be far more effective than ponderous encircling moves by large ones. On one of the former, Captain Oswald Smith-Bingham led a squadron of the Regiment a day's march, which continued through the night without a halt, and captured a Boer convoy at dawn.

Lieutenant Stanley Paddon had a similar, if smaller, success shortly afterwards. Captain Smith-Bingham had earlier been awarded the Distinguished Service Order for leadership during an uncharacteristically close-order combat with some Boers who had attacked the column of which the 3rd were acting as rearguard. He subsequently commanded the Regiment from 1912 until 1916 and retired as a Brigadier-General.

The Commanding Officer from 1897 until 1900 was Colonel Ulick de Burgh who, in 1900, was appointed to command the Commission sent to America to purchase remounts for the war. He and his Commission were responsible for the provision of quality horses which arrived in South Africa before the end of the war. These supplies ensured that the Boers, hemmed in, hungry and exhausted, eventually had no alternative but to surrender.

At the end of 1901 the 3rd were sent to Natal and then to Zululand in pursuit of General Louis Botha, one of the last Boer leaders to be captured. He eluded the column, however, and the Regiment returned to Harrismith in the eastern Orange Free State where, apart from some time spent working on the block-house line, it passed the remainder of the war. The Regiment's casualties for the war were two officers and sixty-one other ranks killed.

6th Dragoon Guards

In 1881 the Regiment had been in Sialkot for a year and remained there until 1885, taking part in exercises aimed at reminding them of the rigours of frontier warfare during winter – the season in which manoeuvres were most comfortably conducted. In March 1885 the Carabiniers participated in a review in Rawalpindi, the Aldershot of India, and the following year changed their station to Mhow, in western central India, where they were warned to prepare themselves for a return home. The Regiment left India from Bombay in October 1888 and arrived at Portsmouth in November. The rapidity of the voyage, made by steamship and via the Suez Canal, indicates just how much of a difference these two factors made to the trip to and from India. On their return home they were two hundred men over their home establishment, and therefore many volunteers had to transfer to the reserve. Cavalry regiments during the 1880s and 1890s operated to one of three establishments: low, medium and high. Eight of those stationed at home in 1898 had to be on high establishment, in order to be ready to move overseas for active service at once. As a newly-returned regiment, the Carabiniers had their establishment progressively cut until, in 1890, the Commanding Officer, Lieutenant-Colonel William MacGeorge, complained that his numbers were so low that the ordinary business of keeping the horses groomed was very difficult, the Regiment having 122 more horses than men.

The Carabiniers moved from Portsmouth to Shorncliffe in Kent on arrival, but were then sent north in 1890 to Birmingham, Bradford and Leeds, where it had become the practice to use soldiers in support of the police during the riots which accompanied strikes and lock-outs in those areas. Remaining in these centres of industrial unrest until 1891, the Regiment was then sent north to Edinburgh, providing an escort to the Queen in Derby on the way, and was quartered in Piershill Barracks, with two troops being detached to Glasgow's Maryhill Barracks. Yorkshire was riven by coal strikes in 1893 and the Carabiniers sent detachments from their station in York to add weight to the police presence in the mining districts. In 1897 the 6th were placed on the higher establishment and, accordingly, received recruits and horses from other regiments. This hint that they were to hold themselves in readiness for an overseas posting bore fruit in 1899 when the South African War began but, in 1897, the increased Regiment formed part of the Aldershot Cavalry Brigade which paraded in review before the Queen to celebrate her Diamond Jubilee.

Mobilisation began on 7 October 1899 and the Regiment was reported as fit for service and ready to embark by 20 October; the war had begun with rejection of a Boer ultimatum on 11 October. Embarking on 3 and 8 November, the two wings of the Carabiniers arrived near Cape Town on 30 November, having lost 22 horses on the voyage out. After only four days' acclimatisation the Regiment was ordered to the front, to Naauwpoort on the northern border of Cape Colony, travelling the 570 miles by troop train. Shortly after they arrived, the war, which had not been going Britain's way at all, dramatically took a turn for the worse with defeats at Stormberg, Magersfontein and Colenso. Ordered to join the cavalry division commanded by Major General John French, the 6th travelled by train from Naauwpoort to attack Boer positions in and around Arundel, south of Colesberg on the border of the Orange Free State. Arundel was occupied on 7 December by the Carabiniers, commanded by Colonel Thomas Porter, and the Regiment then spent some time on patrol along the Arundel to Colesberg railway line, reconnoitring Boer positions but, deliberately, not becoming involved in too much action. This tactic was a result of orders designed to minimise casualties which, because of the Boers' superior marksmanship, tended to be unnecessarily heavy when cavalry attacked Boer positions by frontal assault. On one of these patrols Lieutenant Robert Collis led a small group of men through hostile territory, and so distinguished himself by his concern for their safety when under fire from a party of Boers (whom he had assumed to be friendly), that he was awarded the Distinguished Service Order in 1901. Operations around Colesberg resulted in the town being besieged and the Carabiniers were withdrawn, with the rest of the cavalry, to the relief of Kimberley.

On the way to Kimberley the Regiment was engaged in a number of small actions. In one of these, at Ramah, near the Orange River Station, south of Kimberley and just inside the Orange Free State border, the presence of mind of a Sergeant Bowman prevented the Regiment's Maxim machine-gun from being lost to the Boers. The Carabiniers were placed in the 1st Brigade of the cavalry division, brigaded with the Greys and a squadron of the 6th (Inniskilling) Dragoons, but did not march on Kimberley with the vanguard of the division, being ordered to wait for and escort the transport column. The transport arrived on the night of 13 February 1900 and left immediately, marching through the night towards Kimberley with its escort of Carabiniers. Once the Regiment and the transport reached Klip Drift, on the Modder River twenty-five miles south of Kimberley, it rendezvoused with the remainder of the division and relinquished its escort duties. The division, preceded by its two batteries of horse artillery, marched on Kimberley on 15 February, engaging Boers entrenched north of Klip Drift and carrying the positions with a cavalry charge by brigades, the swiftness of the horses – and the concealing dust that their hooves threw up – making them difficult targets for the Boer marksmen. Total casualties on both sides were relatively small but, seen as a cavalry charge against musketry, the action at Klip Drift came to be regarded, by protagonists of the mounted arm, as a classic example of the correct use of cavalry. It has to be questionable whether the three brigades would have achieved so much without artillery support or the covering nature of dust clouds, but the fact remained that the objective was targeted and overcome in a manner that made John French's reputation as a leader of cavalry. Once the Boers had taken to their heels, the road to Kimberley was open and the Carabiniers led the cavalry's advance on the town. Once the town was occupied Colonel Porter, who had been given command of the 1st Brigade, was made its garrison commander.

The charge at Klip Drift was carried out in true cavalry style, with the front rank of each squadron being armed with lances as well as swords and carbines. This experiment of arming the front rank of all cavalry regiments, except hussars, as lancers, was begun in 1892 as a direct result of the usefulness of the lance in open country and against an unconventional enemy. Although the actual effectiveness of lances was limited, except against dismounted troops or those lying down, the effect on enemy morale seems to have been considerable and so, until the Boer War turned into a manoeuvring stalemate, lances and swords were retained. Once the war had taken that turn, cold steel was returned to the armoury and rifles issued to the cavalry.

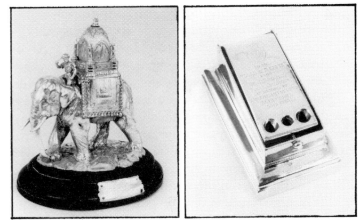

Silver-plated table snuffbox in the form of an elephant and howdah. Presented to the Sergeants' Mess of the Royal Scots Greys by the Non-Commissioned Officers of the 19th Hussars, 18th June 1881. 18 June is the anniversary of the Battle of Waterloo and the elephant, without howdah, was one of the badges of the 19th Hussars, now 15th/19th The King's Royal Hussars.

Silver cigar cutter. Presented to the "Dear Old Greys" from P. J. Browne, Royal Dragoons, in memory of a most pleasant six months, Aldershot, Xmas 1885. *Hallmark: London 1886-87 Maker: R and S Garrard and Co.*

Following the occupation of Kimberley the Boer forces were given little choice but to return to the interior of the Orange Free State. The Boer general, Cronje, headed east from his base at Magersfontein, south of Kimberley, towards Bloemfontein, but was caught up with at Paardeburg, where he was forced to surrender on 27 February 1900 after being bottled up by a series of skirmishing movements on the part of the cavalry. Gradually the Boer forces were forced back along the Modder River towards Bloemfontein, fighting actions at Poplar Grove and Driefontein on the way. At Driefontein Major Alexander Sprot of the Carabiniers led five squadrons under the command of Brigadier-General Robert Broadwood, commanding 2nd Cavalry Brigade, in a charge against entrenched Boer positions which led the Boers to surrender. Bloemfontein was occupied in March and the Boers went over to guerrilla warfare.

The 1st Brigade, still commanded by Colonel Porter of the Carabiniers, spent the next month or so in small reconnaissance operations, which usually resulted in skirmishes of varying sizes. At the beginning of May it formed the advance guard of the main column of an army commanded by Lord Roberts, Commander-in-Chief in South Africa, which left Bloemfontein as part of Roberts's march on Pretoria, the Boer capital. The 1st Cavalry Brigade did not remain all the time with the main army, but spent some time protecting its flanks as it advanced. Action at Virginia Siding, north-east of Bloemfontein, involved A and C squadrons of the Regiment in a concentrated fire-fight in which their carbines were no match for the rifles of the Boers; only the rapid deployment of horse artillery prevented a serious setback. Captain Charles Elworthy, commanding C squadron, and four other ranks were killed during the action, and nine men were wounded.

A week later the Carabiniers occupied the surrendered and evacuated town of Kroonstadt and, on 24 May, the cavalry crossed into the Transvaal, heartland of

Boer territory, of which Pretoria and Johannesburg were the principal cities. Lieutenant William Rundle of the Regiment acted as galloper between the cavalry and the main army under Lord Roberts, still at Kroonstadt. When Roberts was ready to move on Johannesburg, the cavalry led the advance on the left of his army and the Carabiniers encountered little action until 27 May when, at Hartebeestefontein, they attacked Boer positions covering the route to Johannesburg. The town capitulated at the end of May and, with the Regiment as part of the vanguard, the cavalry division moved off towards Pretoria, encountering resistance most of the way. Pretoria surrendered on 5 June and the 1st Cavalry Brigade released 3,500 British prisoners of war incarcerated in Watervaal. Between June and October 1900 the Carabiniers continued their role as reconnaissance troops and skirmishers, being frequently on outpost duty and often in action at all hours with sniping Boers. Lieutenant Noel Calvert, an Australian who had joined the Regiment only six month after rowing in the Cambridge boat during the Boat Race of 1899, was killed when he and a small section of the Regiment, forming part of the rearguard, were ambushed.

In the New Year the Carabiniers left the 1st Cavalry Brigade, which was disbanded as the nature of the war changed from semi-conventional to outright guerrilla, and joined a mixed force commanded by Colonel Edmund Allenby. Allenby's column pursued forces of Boers as fast as it could, but was limited in its effectiveness by its size and by the presence within it of its slow-moving infantry element. Allenby, originally commissioned in 6th (Inniskilling) Dragoons, was a sound, if not spectacular leader of his column. Engaged in gradually mopping up Boer forces, themselves fragmentary, he took few risks but plodded along, never losing an action, and eventually doing just what was wanted: containing the enemy. Exercising the "cavalry spirit" was left to certain of his cavalry officers, most notable among whom was Major Henry Leader of the Carabiniers. Commanding C squadron, Leader lost few opportunities of getting at the enemy, often by forced marches and sudden swoops and, occasionally, by frontal cavalry charges upon entrenched positions. He distinguished himself at Rooi Kraal in February, at Ermelo in April and at Leeufontein in May. As Commanding Officer of 1st Scottish Horse, a better-than-average yeomanry unit, Leader led his new regiment, consisting of four squadrons, in a surprise attack on Gruisfontein in the western Transvaal in February 1902. Complete surprise was achieved and the entire camp of Kommandant Sarel Alberts captured. Leader commanded the Regiment between 1905 and 1909 and was Colonel of the Carabiniers, and Joint Colonel of the combined Regiment, from 1917 until 1925.

The Regiment continued with its rounding-up and containing activities for the remainder of 1901, being involved in fighting at Rietfontein in July and elsewhere in the Transvaal in August and September. Peace was signed at the end of May 1902 and the Regiment left Durban for Madras on 15 August. Its casualties for the war, in which it had been heavily engaged from beginning to end, were six officers and 64 other ranks killed.

Royal Scots Greys

In 1881 the Greys were halfway through a four-year posting to Ireland, returning to Scotland in 1884. In the same year an expedition was mounted from Egypt – which had been temporarily pacified – to go to the rescue of Major General Charles Gordon, who was besieged in Khartoum by the forces of the Mahdi, a Muslim religious leader. General Lord Wolseley of Cairo, who – as Lieutenant-General Sir Garnet Wolseley – had led the Egyptian expedition in 1882, was appointed to lead and co-ordinate the Gordon relief expedition and, as part of his plan, formed a camel corps to act as supporting mounted infantry to his main force, which was to get to Khartoum via the River Nile.

The camel corps had four camel regiments within it, one – the Heavy Camel Regiment – formed of volunteers from, principally, heavy cavalry regiments. To the Heavy Camel Regiment the Greys contributed three officers, two sergeants, two corporals, a trumpeter/bugler and thirty-eight men. Linked with the Greys contingent in the Heavy Camel Regiment were similar-sized contingents from the Household Cavalry, the 2nd, 4th and 5th Dragoon Guards, the 1st Dragoons and the 5th and 16th Lancers. The Greys contingent was commanded by Captain William Hippisley, one of four Greys who had served in the Zulu War of 1879 and who was to command the Regiment from 1900 to 1902. The Heavy Camel Regiment was commanded by Lieutenant-Colonel The Hon. Reginald Talbot of the 1st Life Guards, and the Greys formed part of number four company with the 1st (The Royal) Dragoons. Major Wilfred Gough of the Royals commanded the company and the other Greys officers were Lieutenant Richard Wolfe, who had transferred from 3rd Dragoon Guards in 1878 and who was killed at the Battle of Abu Klea in January 1885, along with twelve other Greys, and Lieutenant William Middleton, who avoided Abu Klea and survived.

The route to Abu Klea was a sandy one and began at Korti, downstream from the fourth cataract on the Nile. Beyond Korti the river swells eastward in a 400-mile bulge, and it was decided that the camel corps and its accompanying units should disembark at Korti and proceed overland by the short-cut, 176 miles, to Metemmeh, ninety-six miles north of Khartoum, where a rendezvous could be effected with the river column. In the afternoon of 30 December 1884 the desert

Silver table centrepiece depicting a sergeant of The Royal Scots Greys and another of the Gordon Highlanders. Presented by the Sergeants 2nd Gordon Highlanders – 92nd – to the Sergeants Royal Scots Greys 1891. *Hallmark: London 1891-92. Maker: Mappin and Webb*

column set off. Gakdul, the halfway point, was reached less than three days later, and the column replenished its water supplies from the Gakdul wells. By 14 January the column, 1,800 strong in terms of troops, had received sufficient supplies to enable it to proceed towards the next wells, at Abu Klea, forty-three miles to the south.

On the 16th, Major John French of the 19th Hussars, reconnoitring ahead, came upon a body of the enemy, Sudan tribesmen, which as he approached revealed itself as an army massed to defend and prevent access to the wells. Accordingly, since night was falling, the column retired into a hastily-constructed *zariba* (thornbush-ringed encampment) and, under sporadic firing, settled down to wait for dawn. As the sun came up, the firing increased and it became apparent that the Sudanese were preparing to attack. The column formed a massive square and advanced.

The square moved forward like a tortoise with a shoe-box-shaped shell. The Heavy Camel Regiment formed the rear side, number five company (16th and 5th Lancers) taking the place of the near hind leg, and where the tail would be was the Naval Brigade with its Gardner gun – a British version of the Gatling machine-gun. Number four company (Royals and Greys) was around the corner next to number five company, and had on its left number three company (4th and 5th Dragoon Guards), which was flanked by the Naval Brigade. In the centre of the square were the camels, the soldiers having dismounted for ease of manoeuvre.

As it moved ponderously forward the square presented a large and slow-moving target for the enemy riflemen, and many casualties resulted as the square

Silver eagle toothpick holder, representative of the eagle captured at Waterloo. Presented to the Sergeants' Mess, Royal Scots Greys, by Lt. Colonel Maberley, on his retiring from the command of the Regiment 1892. *The neck of the eagle is hinged and opens to reveal the toothpick receptacle. Hallmark: London 1892-93. Maker: Chapple and Mantell*

gradually became an oblong, stretched by the inability of the camels in the centre to keep pace or formation. As the wounded began to increase, the rear side of the square became ragged and, as the enemy's fire increased from the square's left rear quarter, the sides of the formation became distorted, encouraging number four company to reinforce the left face. After a march in this haphazard – if not ludicrous – fashion, the Sudanese seemed about to attack and so the square halted. This movement left several camels outside the square, with their burden of wounded soldiers. The square was weakened in its left rear corner (the position of the Greys) by the unthinking gallantry of several soldiers breaking ranks and collecting the camels and their wounded comrades. Seeing the danger Lord Charles Beresford, commanding the Naval Brigade, ordered the Gardner gun to be wheeled out of the square and turned on the advancing tribesmen. The gun jammed after seventy rounds and all its crew, except Beresford and a rating, were cut to pieces. At the same time the Sudanese rushed the left face of the square. Seeking to recover both the gun and a body of skirmishers who had been exchanging pot shots with the tribesmen outside the square, number three company were ordered to wheel back to let them in. In less time than it takes to read about it, the Sudanese were inside the incomplete square and being reinforced each second by fresh, frenzied waves. Fortunately for the survival of the entire column, the barrier presented by the mass of phlegmatic camels in the centre of the square prevented total chaos from ensuing. The rapid about-face of

Silver-mounted ram's horn table snuff mull.
Presented to the Royal Scots Greys from Majors Heath, K.O.
Yorksh. L.I., Adye, R. Irish Rifles, and Douglas, Royal Scots;
Captains Sandbach, R.E., Stopford, Derbysh. Regt., Phillips,
Welsh Regt., and MacDonogh, R.E., attached from Staff
College, May 1896. *Hallmark: Edinburgh 1895-96. Maker:
Hamilton and Inches*

the rear ranks of the troops in the opposite corner to the ill-advised opening
resulted in a slaughter of tribesmen, especially once the square closed and they had
no way out. The entire battle is thought to have taken ten minutes; enemy
casualties were estimated at 800 dead, British ones computed at seventy-six killed
and ninety-two wounded. By mid March 1885, having discovered Gordon dead,
the expedition had returned to Korti and re-embarked.

While their small detachment were experiencing such excitement in the Sudan,
the remainder of the Regiment stayed in Edinburgh, marching south to Aldershot
in 1886. After a spell in Brighton in 1888, the Greys returned to Ireland until 1894.
In December of that year, in line with similar appointments made in other
distinguished cavalry regiments, the Queen appointed His Imperial Majesty
Nicholas II, Tsar of All the Russias, to be the first Colonel-in-Chief of the
Regiment. At that time few regiments had Colonels-in-Chief, and the
appointment reflected not only the affection that the Queen had for the
Regiment, but also her friendship towards the Tsar and his interest in the Scots
Greys. From 1895 to 1897 the Regiment remained in southern England, in
Hounslow and Aldershot, but spent 1898 and the greater part of 1899 in
Edinburgh.

The Greys were ordered to mobilise for service in South Africa on 7 September
1899 and reported that mobilisation was complete on 17 October. The
Headquarters and B squadron embarked first, on 5 November from Glasgow. A
and C squadrons had to exchange their horses for others owing to an outbreak of
the equine ailment "pink-eye", but C squadron left Edinburgh on 16 November,
took over undiseased horses in Aldershot, and sailed from Southampton. A
squadron left Edinburgh the next day, took over a squadron of horses from 17th
(Duke of Cambridge's Own) Lancers, and all the squadrons were united near
Cape Town on 8 December.

For the first two months of their time in South Africa the Regiment operated by

Silver cup.
Challenge Cup for best shot amongst the members of the Sergeants' Mess, Third Dragoon Guards. Presented by Lt. Colonel R.K. Parke, commanding the Third Dragoon Guards 1892. *Hallmark: London 1895-96. Maker: Mappin and Webb*

Set of four silver-gilt table lighters in the form of flaming grenades or bombs. Presented to the Royal Scots Greys by Kaiser Wilhelm II, Emperor of Germany, Aldershot, 1894. In unhallmarked German silver-gilt, the form of these lighters commemorates the use of the flaming grenade as a badge by the Greys. Each lighter contains a reservoir of methylated spirits and three individual torches.

squadrons, principally based on and around the Orange River station in the north of Cape Colony. When the cavalry division was organised in February 1900, the Greys formed part of the 1st Cavalry Brigade, with the Carabiniers and 6th (Inniskilling) Dragoons. The Regiment's experiences between February 1900 and the capture of Pretoria on 5 June were broadly similar to those of the Carabiniers, sketched in above. The Greys participated in the cavalry charge at Klip Drift, losing two soldiers – Privates 3354 Sutherland and 3237 McGinn – wounded and at the siege and Battle of Paardeburg. A short action was fought at Dronfield on 16 February, when three other ranks were killed and seven of all ranks wounded, Second Lieutenant The Hon. William McClintock Bunbury subsequently dying from his wounds. The front rank of the Greys surrendered its lances on 6 March, before the action at Poplar Grove, and sustained two wounded other ranks – Sergeant Trumpeter 2423 Inkster and Private 4394 Harris – at Driefontein on 10 March.

Major Henry Scobell and C squadron charged and assaulted a Boer position west of Bloemfontein on 12 March, Scobell adding to a growing reputation that was to make him a Major General in 1903, commanding the 1st Cavalry Brigade in Aldershot. Four months later, owing to bad communications, Major Scobell and his command of three companies of the Suffolk Regiment, together with C squadron of the Greys, were forced to surrender at Zilikat's Nek, west of Pretoria. Major Scobell escaped the same evening and walked back to Pretoria. By June 1901 he was commanding a fast-moving column of over a thousand men and was well on the way to stardom.

At the end of January 1901 the 1st Cavalry Brigade was disbanded and, coincidentally but propitiously, carbines were replaced by Lee Enfield rifles. For the type of anti-guerrilla warfare that was about to involve them, the Regiment needed the extra range that the rifle provided over the carbine. Occupied in the eastern Transvaal, as part of an eight-column force commanded by French, the Greys marched back and forth, escorting convoys, carrying out skirmishing operations and, in March 1901, having C squadron linked to a squadron of the Carabiniers for two small raids which netted guns and ammunition from the Boers. In April the Greys column was placed under the command of Colonel Edmund Allenby and so was closely involved, in the remaining months of the war, with the Carabiniers as part of Allenby's encircling movement against the remaining Boer forces.

By the end of the war the Regiment had lost seven officers and sixty-seven men killed or died, and four officers and eighty-two men wounded. The Greys remained in South Africa after the end of the war, receiving Colonel Henry Scobell as their Commanding Officer in 1902.

CHAPTER SIX
In Flanders Fields

1903-1922

3rd Dragoon Guards

The 3rd remained in South Africa until 1904, when they moved to Ireland. In 1903 Lieutenant-Colonel Francis Garratt of the Carabiniers was appointed to the command of the Regiment for a year, after which he left to command the Carabiniers. Garratt had made a name for himself during the Boer War as a leader of irregular regiments of cavalry and had been made a Companion of the Order of the Bath and awarded the Distinguished Service Order; he retired as a Brigadier-General.

Nothing of note is recorded as having happened to the Regiment in Ireland during the four years of its tour of duty there, and it was posted to England for a further four years in 1908 before handing over its horses to the Carabiniers on their return home, and moving to Egypt in 1912. In 1910, apparently, the Regiment had managed to match its horses' colour by troop – blacks, bays and chestnuts, with probably greys retained for the band. Although many changes in the art of war and training were achieved too during the years between the ending of the Boer War and the collapse of the Edwardian twilight in 1914, the importance of keeping up appearances was not uncharacteristic of the British cavalry's attitude to soldiering in the decade prior to the First World War.

Professionalism was on the increase in the Army during the first decade of the twentieth century, and some of the easier lessons of the Boer War were learnt. Unfortunately, few in authority contemplated that the next war might be larger in scale than the Boer War, might not be fought in terrain where the cavalry could be given full rein, or might be against a rather better-organised army than that which the Boers had been able to field. Those who did identify Germany as the likely enemy and Europe as the likely theatre of operations were either unaware of the likelihood of stalemate under battlefield conditions or too junior to have their

Silver cup, the Cavalry Cup.
Presented by Col. H. Mercer to the NCOs and Men, 3rd Dragoon Guards, to commemorate winning The Cavalry Cup 1905-08, four years of his command. *Hallmark: London 1896-97. Maker: William Hutton and Sons Ltd.*

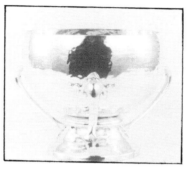

Silver cup, the Sykes Cup. For the best trained remount 3rd Dragoon Guards. Awarded 1907-13 and 1923. Hallmark: Dublin 1906-07. Maker: West and Son

views heeded. While army reforms were wide-ranging and resulted in the British Army which went to France in 1914 being, without doubt, the best fed, led and organised army which Britain had ever sent overseas, the nature of the campaign which resulted for the next four years was largely unforeseen. This is not altogether surprising, even if one considers empirical knowledge as the only valid kind, since no British soldier then in a position of influence had fought a cavalry action in northern Europe. Eminent cavalry soldiers in the Army, such as Douglas Haig and John French, had campaigned in Egypt, the Sudan, India and South Africa. There, the terrain was open, the opposition – although numerous – was poorly-organised, under-weaponed and generally devoid of machine-guns. Kitchener, who as a young Woolwich cadet had seen the Franco-Prussian War of 1870-71 at close quarters, had failed to appreciate the effect of the machine-gun against cavalry because it was rarely used as other than a piece of long-distance artillery. The effectiveness of the Boers' machine-guns had been negated both by the speed of the cavalry and by the fact that these weapons were rudimentary in comparison to those which would figure in such large numbers in the German Army of 1914.

Few soldiers writing at the time, or in positions of senior command, seem to have considered for a moment an alternative view to the one loudly and frequently proclaimed, that the traditional role of the cavalry would play a considerable and significant part in the war to come. Kitchener and Roberts, both from backgrounds unlikely to have equipped either with a high regard for the cavalry spirit, saw a little way through the pro-cavalry arguments, but not far enough. Roberts was instrumental in abolishing the lance in 1903, except for ceremonial occasions, but he was largely ignored, and it was reinstated in 1909. All were agreed, however, that the cavalry's marksmanship needed improvement,

Skill at Arms Challenge Cup. Presented by Maj. R.E. McHomer, 3rd Dragoon Guards, 1913 for NCO or Man between 4 or 8 years' service making highest aggregate in Regimental sports. *Hallmark: Sheffield 1911-12. Maker: Walker and Hall.*

Silver table lighter in the form of a ship's capstan. Presented to the Officers, Third Dragoon Guards, from their Naval guests, Cairo, November 1913. *Hallmark: London 1913-14. Maker: Page, Keen and Page.*

and this was slowly attended to, aided by the issue (from 1903) of the short magazine Lee Enfield rifle to both infantry and cavalry; no longer would the mounted arm have to put up with the carbine. In 1908 the question of cut or thrust for the sword was finally decided and a new pattern sword issued which, with its long, needle-like blade, was good only for the thrust, such as would take place during an in-line cavalry charge. Its embellished version is the pattern still carried by most cavalry officers, for whom it was introduced in 1912. While being, without doubt, one of the finest cavalry swords ever designed, it must be regarded as ironic that it was introduced at a time when its use was decreasing and was shortly to vanish.

The 3rd Dragoon Guards were still in Egypt when war broke out in August 1914, and were quartered on the outskirts of Cairo. Egypt, flanking the Suez Canal, was regarded as a vital possession guarding the route to India and, while Turkey's intentions remained unknown in the early months of the year, it had to be defended against possible Turkish incursion from its colonies to the north and east. The Regiment, while it awaited relief by yeomanry forces from home, remained guarding the canal until the end of September 1914, when it embarked for England, arriving in Liverpool in mid-October.

Both World Wars were to be notable for the extent to which regimental identities were rapidly submerged beneath the much larger identities of Brigades, Divisions and Army Corps. Accordingly, the 3rd were placed in the 6th Cavalry Division, being brigaded with 1st (Royal) Dragoons and 10th (Prince of Wales's Own) Hussars, both of which regiments preceded the 3rd to France and were involved in the 1st Battle of Ypres in late October. The Regiment eventually sailed for France on 31 October and were in the line, dismounted, by 5 November.

For the next fortnight they held their position, against assault after assault of German troops attempting to break through to Ypres. Their positions, shallowly-entrenched and rapidly becoming waterlogged, were repeatedly shelled and – the art of entrenching being in its infancy – many troopers were killed by snipers as they attempted to move around. For their services in the trenches at the first Battle of Ypres, eight officers and men were mentioned in dispatches and Captain Edwin Wright, who had led an attack on an enemy-held farmhouse that was acting as a strongpoint, and who had shot four Germans dead with his service revolver, was recommended – unsuccessfully – for the posthumous award of a Victoria Cross; he had been killed after the farm was occupied. On 20 November the Regiment was relieved and spent much of the rest of the winter in billets behind the lines, occasionally supplying working parties or hastily-required reinforcements for the front.

The 3rd returned to the trenches at Zillebeke in front of Ypres on 8 February 1915 and remained there until the 13th, being relieved by the Carabiniers. At the 2nd Battle of Ypres in April 1915 the Germans used poison gas for the first time and, as a result, penetrated far into the British positions. The 3rd were kept in reserve throughout the battle, constantly mounted and moving from position to position as the situation demanded and as the line weakened in various places. At the beginning of May, after a ferocious German counter-attack, the 3rd were moved back into the line to relieve the King's Shropshire Light Infantry, one of the many infantry regiments which had borne the brunt of the fighting in the trenches. The trenches that the Regiment occupied had been hastily dug, were hardly two feet deep and without sandbags, and there were no communication trenches; in an overnight lull the relieving forces busied themselves in reconstructing and reinforcing the defences. At dawn on 15 May the entire line was heavily shelled as a preamble to a massed infantry attack, part of which broke through on A squadron's left, almost encircling them. The battle ebbed and flowed with advances and retreats over a few yards of ground to left and right, but eventually the original positions were regained. Further fighting took place during the following few days and the Regiment was relieved by the 20th Hussars on 20 May, returning to its billets behind the lines. Three days later it was back in the Ypres Salient, defending the Château at Hooge until 4 June, ten days in which it was subjected to fearsome bombardments and successive waves of German infantry. The 3rd's casualties were severe, as a result of its participation in the 2nd Battle of Ypres, twenty-five officers and men were awarded gallantry distinctions, varying from eleven mentions in dispatches, through five Military Medals and five Distinguished Conduct Medals to two Military Crosses and a Distinguished Service Order.

Until 20 August 1915 the Regiment remained in billets behind the line, training, testing gas masks, perfecting machine-gun drill and playing polo. The 3rd

Silver tray.
Presented to the Sergeants, 3rd (Prince of Wales's) Dragoon
Guards by the Sergeants 2nd Bn. The Gordon Highlanders, As a
Memoir of their Comradeship, Cairo 1913-14. *Hallmark: Sheffield
1913-14. Maker: James Dixon and Sons.*

reconnoitred positions behind the infantry, which had won the initial engagement
at the Battle of Loos, and with them were ordered forward, dismounted, first to
occupy the deserted German trenches and then to occupy Loos itself. The
Regiment and its accompanying infantry occupied the village and entrenched
themselves rapidly, while under constant shell-fire. From their positions they
were able to support the advancing infantry and, the battle won, were withdrawn
at the end of September.

After spending the winter in billets behind the line, a dismounted company of
the 3rd were brought forward again in January 1916 to Vermelles, where they
remained, seeing a little action, until 8 February, when they were withdrawn.
Little of great consequence happened in the Regiment in 1916 prior to the Battle
of the Somme, which began in July and which most cavalry regiments believed, or
hoped at least, would provide the break-out for which the cavalry waited during
the entire course of the war. As is now well known, the colossal butcher's bill of
the Somme provided no such opportunity for the Regiment, who were barely
involved and remained largely out of serious action until well into 1917.

In April 1917 the Regiment was ordered to advance to Arras and did so
mounted, only dismounting as they neared the front lines, near Monchy-le-
Preux, a village which they were ordered to attack. The attack proceeded, under
bombardment and, eventually, after a series of counter-attacks against the
Regiment's B and C squadrons, the 3rd gained and held its positions until relieved
on the evening of 11 April 1917. Between May and June sections of trenches in the
line at Epehy were occupied by the Regiment, but they were then relieved, in time
to participate in the cavalry corps horse show in July. At Cambrai in November
the Regiment contributed nine officers and 218 other ranks to a dismounted
division which took over a section of the front line threatened by a German
counter-attack following the earlier successes of the tanks.

The winter of 1917-18 was relatively quiet for the Regiment and it, like so many
of its fellow regiments, was taken by surprise by the strength of the German

offensive of 1918, which erupted in March when the 3rd were in quarters in Devise. Although a measure of confusion resulted and the greater part of the Army retired, the Regiment went into action in its dismounted role once the retreat had ceased and defensible positions had been reached. On several occasions over the next two or three days, the Regiment found itself all but surrounded by German forces which had advanced at some speed, one German attack on the village of Viry-Noureuil succeeding in capturing the officers' mess, although not without a sustained argument from the staff. The line having been secured, the dismounted troopers rejoined the cavalry and withdrew. At the same time as their comrades were fighting as efficiently as infantrymen, a mounted troop of the 3rd, commanded by Lieutenant Arthur Vincent, formed part of a cavalry charge against bodies of German infantrymen occupying a pair of copses near the village of Villeselve. The 3rd charged the right copse, across ploughed land and in the face of rifle and machine-gun fire, which caused them to complete the charge in extended line and – at the cost of seventy-five casualties – carry the position.

For the remainder of the war, the Regiment was both split and united, mounted and dismounted by troop and by squadron, and formed part of the final offensive advance that eventually won back all the ground lost in March and April 1918. In October 1918 a German position at Honnechy was seriously impeding the westward advance of the British, and the 6th Cavalry Brigade were ordered to assault it. The 3rd formed the right of the advance and rode for two miles, under constant enfilade machine-gun fire from German positions on their right, but took the village with minimal casualties. The charge at Honnechy finished the 3rd's contribution to the First World War, a campaign that had involved 1,816 officers and men of the Regiment, 951 of whom became casualties; the highest number of casualties suffered by any regular cavalry regiment.

Throughout the early months of 1919 the process of demobilisation continued, and was completed on 7 March. Reduced to cadre strength of ninety-nine of all ranks, the Regiment left Antwerp on 22 March, reached Southampton on 25 March and arrived at Assaye Barracks, Tidworth, the same evening. Later in the year the Regiment was posted to India, being stationed at Sialkot. By 1922 it had been reduced to two squadrons in preparation for its amalgamation with the Carabiniers.

6th Dragoon Guards

On arrival in India in the autumn of 1902, the strength of the Carabiniers was

The charge of the 3rd Dragoon Guards at Honnechy, 9 October 1918. Presented to the Regiment by Major H.P. Holt MC. Artist: Lionel Edwards (1878-1966).

increased by drafts from the 1st and the 3rd Dragoon Guards to raise it to the Indian establishment of 627 of all ranks. After four years in Bangalore the 6th moved to Mhow in 1906, having received a new standard from HRH The Prince of Wales, later King George V, earlier in the year. After two years in Mhow it was moved to South Africa, to relieve the 5th Dragoon Guards at Bloemfontein in 1908. Two years later it left South Africa and came home, to take over the 3rd Dragoon Guards' horses in Canterbury.

The Regiment mobilised in four days in August 1914, its preparedness – like that of most of the rest of the Army – being due to the fact that it had been obvious that war was on the way for about a fortnight before the first of the German Army crossed the Belgian frontier and committed Britain to fighting.

The causes of the First World War had, like those of the Indian Mutiny, which had also involved the Carabiniers, evolved over several decades by the time that the Archduke Franz Ferdinand, son of the Emperor of Austria, was shot dead by a Serbian terrorist in Sarajevo in July 1914. By 1871 Germany had finally established herself as the strongest power in Europe, having brushed Denmark aside in 1863, humiliated Austrian and Bavarian forces in 1866 and trounced those of France in 1870-71. Strength in Europe counted for very little without domination of the seas, however, as Bonaparte had eventually discovered, and Germany's warship-building programme of the 1890s and 1900s finally awoke Britain to the threat posed by her increasingly assertive neighbour. In what generations of schoolboys have come to learn about as "the scramble for Africa", the European powers competed with indelicate, but entirely typical, haste for a slice of that continent; Germany – which started late – getting least of all the major contenders. Tacit German support for the Boers in South Africa had set Britain's teeth on edge. Despite the German Kaiser's avowed respect for so many British institutions (he was Colonel-in-Chief of 1st (Royal) Dragoons 1894-1914), it gradually became clear that Britain would have to fight Germany. The position was not helped by France's anti-German paranoia or, indeed, by that of Russia, which felt threatened by a powerful neighbour to her west, and Britain had been linked by alliances with these prickly powers for several years by 1914. Once Russia had declared war in support of Serbia (which was being bullied by Austria), France and Germany rushed to their allies' aid, and when Belgian neutrality was violated by the German invasion, Britain felt compelled to intervene.

The Carabiniers left Canterbury ten days after the declaration of war, and was brigaded with a composite Household Cavalry regiment and the 3rd (King's Own) Hussars within the 4th Cavalry Brigade of the cavalry division. The division was commanded by Major General Edmund Allenby, who had formed such a high opinion of the Carabiniers during the Boer War.

Belgium rapidly collapsed under the German advance, and the British Expeditionary Force (BEF) fell back before it, fighting rearguard actions at Mons, Le Cateau and Guise. Eventually a line was held on the River Marne, which prevented German forces reaching Paris and ending the war, as Germany had planned, in six weeks. Several mounted engagements were fought in the early weeks of the war, while the war was still one of movement, and successes were claimed by the Carabiniers in cavalry actions against German Cuirassiers and Uhlans (lancers). The 4th Cavalry Brigade was ordered to hold the Mons-Condé Canal against a German assault, and the Carabiniers were given two crossing-points, at lock five, east of Condé, and at Albert, to defend. Until being relieved by the Middlesex Regiment on the evening of 26 August, the Regiment held its position on the west bank of the canal, inflicting severe casualties on the German infantry which attempted to cross it in massed waves. After withdrawal to billets

Bronze statuette of a charging cavalry trooper and Highlander, in uniforms of the 1914-16 period. This is clearly a modern allegory of the "stirrup charge" of the Gordons and Greys at Waterloo; it does not commemorate an actual event.
Maker unknown

behind the line, the brigade covered the general retreat from Mons which was necessary to avoid the BEF being encircled as the Germans cut through the fleeing French armies on the British flank. Further cavalry actions were fought during the withdrawal as the Carabiniers protected the withdrawing rear of the British infantry. By penetrating so far south, the German forces had, themselves, been in danger of being cut off by British and French forces on their flanks and, as the advance from the Marne gathered speed, so the German armies fell back before it. In this rapid advance against the withdrawing enemy, the cavalry division was frequently employed in riding down unsupported artillery trains or cutting off isolated bodies of infantry; cavalry-to-cavalry engagements were fought too as the British advance gathered speed, almost outstripping the French. The Germans finally halted on the River Aisne, where the beginnings of the trench warfare were observed as they dug in, in the face of strong British and French forces which attempted to cross the river. At the beginning of October British forces on the Aisne were relieved by the French, and the BEF moved north at some speed to race the Germans to the Channel ports and prevent them from turning the Allied flank. By 19 October the BEF was in the position that it was to occupy for most of the remainder of the war, on the left of the Allied line, with Belgian and French forces between it and the sea, and centred upon Ypres.

A salient was formed around Ypres which was actually a bulge in the Allied line, its configuration meaning that the Germans were able to fire into it from three sides. For some time, too, the British in the salient were below German forces on surrounding ridges, which meant that the enemy had a great advantage in observing the damage that their shelling was doing to British positions. British casualties in the Ypres salient were, not surprisingly, considerable. The

Carabiniers fought dismounted in the rapidly-growing trench system in the salient in various sectors during the 1st Battle of Ypres, holding part of the line at Messines and being almost surrounded by German advances on 1 November 1914.

The Carabiniers relieved the 3rd Dragoon Guards south-east of Ypres in January 1915 and were, in turn, relieved by the Greys on 18 February, moving to billets in Ypres. The Carabiniers were little involved in the 2nd Battle of Ypres but, during a short spell in the trenches in April 1915, claimed a shot-down German aircraft, from which the pilot and observer were captured. The remainder of 1915 was quiet for the Regiment.

Throughout the Somme offensive of mid-1916 the Carabiniers' experiences were similar to those of the 3rd Dragoon Guards, being moved about and waiting for an exploitable gap to open in the German lines. With the unbreakable stalemate of the increasingly sophisticated type of trench warfare that was being waged by 1916, there was little opportunity for the "traditional" use of cavalry and, although the Regiment provided dismounted drafts to reinforce sectors in the front line, little else of any consequence was recorded.

The Regiment remained in reserve during the Battle of Arras in 1917 although, after the initial success brought by the battle, they occupied trenches in the line to relieve the exhausted infantry, on whom the brunt of the fighting had fallen. Further, relatively uneventful, activities in the trenches continued, with regular reliefs, until March 1918, when the last major German offensive of the war began.

At the beginning of the offensive, the Carabiniers were encamped, resting and training, at Grandru, and had been warned to expect the offensive, unlike the 3rd Dragoon Guards. Dismounted sections of the Regiment were detailed to hold the line as the offensive continued, and did so under conditions of increasing chaos until it was forced to withdraw from its position on the Mennisis Canal. As the offensive began to collapse, so gaps opened in the German lines, and what had been a retreat turned gradually into an advance, as – momentarily – a war of stalemate became one of movement. Like the 3rd Dragoon Guards, the Carabiniers were able to fight several mounted actions as their speed on horses enabled them quickly to exploit splits and tears in the German defences. All was not unbroken advance, though, and on occasions when the French on the flanks had given way in the face of German assaults, it often became necessary for the cavalry division to pull back rather than leave their flanks exposed to enemy attacks. At Cuy a squadron of the Regiment, together with one of 1st (Royal) Dragoons and 3rd Dragoon Guards, held a break in the line against heavy attacking German forces, thus covering the retirement to Dives.

For the remainder of 1918 the Carabiniers performed mounted and

Elephant's foot wastepaper bin with a plated rim inscribed: Dem Offizierkorps des Königs-Ulanen-Regiments (1 Hannoverschen) No. 13 widmet diese seine Jagd-Trophaee aus Ceylon zur freundlichen Erinnerung sein einstiger Kamerad Franz von Veltheim-Harbke, Rittmeister A.D.. Ein Horrido den Königs Ulanen! *Translation: This hunting trophy is dedicated to the Officers of 13th King's Uhlans (1st Hanoverian) in friendly commemoration of their former comrade, Captain Franz von Veltheim-Harbke, retired. A tallyho for the King's Uhlans! Presumably a trophy from the First World War. Franz von Veltheim was born in Ostrau, Saxony, in 1848 and joined his regiment in 1868, being adjutant between 1870 and 1871. He retired to the reserve in 1873.*

dismounted duties in conjunction with the infantry, resisting the final German offensive in July and participating in the Allied attack at Amiens in August which effectively brought the German government to the negotiating table. At the end of August the Regiment provided detachments for the 17th and 35th Infantry Divisions, their function being to act in reconnaissance role and as gallopers between units. The Carabiniers ended their war in Belgium as the rest of the Army marched into Germany to enforce the armistice.

The Regiment suffered 265 casualties during the war, 140 of whom were killed, died of wounds or were posted missing. Forty-nine officers and men were mentioned in dispatches and a large number of decorations for gallantry were awarded.

The Carabiniers left Belgium in March 1919 and moved to join the Army of Occupation in Germany for six months before being posted to Ireland in September 1919.

For the last three years of its separate existence, the Regiment was actively engaged in Ireland in the counter-insurgency operations against the forces of the Irish Republican Army. The campaign in Ireland was ideally suited to the cavalry, but the IRA's intelligence system was such that moves against its bands were frustrated. Confronted by an unwinnable campaign – and one of which public opinion had finally had enough – British forces were withdrawn in 1922. The Irish Free State was established and partitioned from six of the nine counties of the province of Ulster, which retained their parliamentary links with mainland Britain.

Widespread reforms and economies in the Army during the 1920s led to large numbers of amalgamations in the British and Indian armies and, being the most expensive arm of both armies, the cavalry was reduced to about half its former number of regiments. The Carabiniers were ordered to reduce establishment to one squadron and proceed to India to be amalgamated with the 3rd Dragoon Guards.

Royal Scots Greys

Remaining in Cape Colony until 1904, the Greys returned to Britain in that year and stayed at home, stationed in various areas of Britain, until the outbreak of the First World War. The Edwardian years were much the same for the Greys as they were for any other British, or indeed Indian, cavalry regiment which saw no active service. Training and various forms of recreation, together with the changes in the Army sketched out above, occupied their time, but not to the extent that the Regiment's efficiency as a fighting unit was impaired. Demonstrating this is the fact that mobilisation, when ordered on 3 August 1914, was achieved by the Greys by the 8th.

The Regiment formed part of the 5th Cavalry Brigade, with 12th (The Prince of Wales's Royal) Lancers and 20th Hussars as the rest of the cavalry element. The brigade was commanded by Brigadier-General Sir Philip Chetwode, later a Field Marshal, peer, father-in-law of the poet Sir John Betjeman and Colonel of the Regiment from 1925 to 1947. The Greys arrived in France on 18 August and were moved up to the Belgian border to await the inevitable onslaught.

One of the earliest tasks which the Greys, alone of all the British cavalry regiments, had to undertake was the camouflaging of their horses. As a regiment of greys, any observer seeing them all together in the line would easily be able to know which regiment was positioned there and, by extrapolation from the barely secret Order of Battle, be able to work out what other regiments were likely to be in the vicinity. This task had been carried out in South Africa and consisted of staining the horses with a proprietorial preparation of permanganate of potash known as Condy's Fluid. As long as the horses remained relatively unsweated and not rained upon, the resulting chestnut colour was reputed to last about a month. How the horses felt about it is not recorded, nor is whether, as a counter-intelligence move, other regiments positioned elsewhere were instructed to dye their horses grey. Properly camouflaged, the Regiment waited on the Belgian border near Binches, between Charleroi and Mons, on the extreme right of the British Expeditionary Force.

After a series of minor engagements with the enemy, principally as the Germans advanced comparatively slowly in a series of connected feints, testing the defences before them, the Regiment fell back with the remainder of the cavalry to cover the retreat from Mons to the Marne. The retreat happened so fast, and involved such confusion, that it is not surprising that the Regiment temporarily mislaid one of its French interpreters, a volunteer called Paul Maze (who later became a distinguished artist). Maze awoke in a village to find that the Greys had left and that it was occupied by Uhlans; escaping, he made his way in the

Silver statuette, the Sprot Cup.
Point to Point challenge trophy presented by Lieut. Mark Sprot, Royal Scots Greys, 1906. *The heron and motto:* Parce qu'il me plaît, *are the crest and motto of the Sprot family. This cup is competed for when the Regiment is stationed in Britain. Hallmark: London 1905-06. Maker: Goldsmiths' and Silversmiths' Company Ltd.*

Silver three-handled cup.
Presented to The Warrant Officers, Staff Sergeants and Sergeants, Royal Scots Greys, by a few Honorary Members and Friends of the Mess, as a Mark of Esteem on their leaving Edinburgh, May 1907. *Hallmark: Chester 1906-07 Maker: Walker and Hall*

general direction of the retreat, only to be arrested by the British on suspicion of being a spy. About to be shot as such, without trial, he was recognised by Major Foster Swetenham, commanding C squadron, as the Regiment passed through the village where he was under guard, and rejoined the Greys. Swetenham was killed a couple of hours after saving Maze's life, in a brief but bloody engagement between the Regiment and a force of German cavalry which were seeking to surround part of the rearguard of the retreat. Maze dedicated his book *A Frenchman in Khaki* to the officer who had saved his life so fortuitously, but shortly afterwards he left the Regiment to be attached as an interpreter to the British Army staff.

After helping to cover the retreat to the Marne, the Greys – as part of the 5th Cavalry Brigade – led the British 2nd Army Corps in the advance from the Marne to the Aisne. Once that river was crossed and the French established upon it in strength, the 5th Brigade led the BEF again in the hundred-mile dash to Amiens as part of the race with the Germans to the coast. From Amiens the BEF turned

Two silver cups, 2nd Cavalry Division Horse Show.
Left: Section 4 of horses on active service from Aug. 1914 to May 1916. Winners Royal Scots Greys. Presented by Major General Sir Philip Chetwode Bart. CB DSO (commanding 2nd Cav. Div.) France 1916. *Hallmark: Birmingham 1915-16. Maker unidentified.*

Right: Best troop of turnout horses, won by 1st troop A squadron (Royal Scots Greys), France 1917. *Hallmark: London 1914-15. Maker: Goldsmiths' and Silversmiths' Company Ltd.*

north-west until joined in mid October by the 3rd Cavalry Division who had recently arrived on the Western Front.

During the 1st Battle of Ypres the Greys occupied trenches and fought as infantry, as did the majority of the cavalry in that sector. The soldiers rapidly became used to their bayonets, to which they resorted far more than their swords during the battle, causing large casualties among the waves of advancing Germans by the accuracy of their musketry. Their last action of note in 1914 was that at Wytschaete, where C squadron continued in action, pouring volley after volley into the advancing German infantry, until the troop leaders were forcibly restrained and ordered to retire by the Commanding Officer, who was about to hand over the position to the French.

Throughout the second year of the war, the Greys alternated duties between spells in the trenches and spells behind the lines, resting and training. In this, their experience was little different to that of any other British cavalry regiment. The stalemate nature of the war had been recognised, if not accepted, and so – while horses were retained both as part of the training process and in the event of an opportunity arising to use them – the Greys and their fellow cavalry regiments were increasingly trained to be infantry, including grenade-training among their acquired skills. The Regiment was stationed beside the Carabiniers during the 2nd Battle of Ypres in April 1915 where – fortunately, since no gas masks had been issued – they avoided the effects of the Germans' first gas attack.

Earlier in April the 2nd Cavalry Division had held a horse show at which the Regiment had carried off three first prizes. These shows were to be repeated in 1916 and 1917, and two of the silver cups that were awarded at these latter events are now in the possession of the sergeants' mess. Events of this kind, which only in their equestrian nature were unique to the cavalry, were relatively common throughout periods of the war when the front was quiet and when bodies of

Silver rosebowl.
Presented to Captain K. McKenzie from the Officers, Royal Scots Greys, July 18th 1914. *Engraved with twenty-nine signatures, this was probably a wedding present. Hallmark: London 1913-14. Maker: C C Pilling for Sibray Hall and Company Ltd.*

Silver frame for Hunting appointments.
Presented to Lieut. Colonel A.D. Miller DSO and officers of the Royal Scots Greys from E. Rube, Royal Dragoons, 1907. *Hallmark: London 1907-08. Maker: Goldsmiths' and Silversmiths' Company Ltd*

troops could be withdrawn for rest and recuperation. An event which was believed to be unique to the Greys was the officers' celebration of Waterloo Day, 18 June, when twenty-three of them, and the Medical Officer, celebrated the hundredth anniversary of the battle with dinner at Staple.

At the end of 1915 the Greys provided a dismounted company to serve in a battalion of dismounted cavalry intended for frequent postings to the trenches. In the first five weeks of their service the Greys' dismounted company sustained sixty-five casualties, most from the effects of having a mine exploded beneath their trenches.

For the Greys, as for the remainder of the cavalry, 1916 was a year of some inaction and, as a result, considerable frustration at the lack of opportunity for mounted warfare in the absence of the expected breakthroughs after the Battle of the Somme. Steel helmets were issued for the first time; resembling inverted soup-plates, they did not greatly appeal to the traditionalists. However, while a Greys trooper, McConnachie (probably the squadron comedian), was larking about with one on, he sustained a direct hit from a piece of anti-aircraft shrapnel and lived, with nothing worse than a headache. Learning from Trooper McConnachie's experience, the Regiment readily adopted the steel helmet, emblazoning it with yellow saltires and, later, with printed symbols indicating squadron allegiances.

1917, like 1916, promised well for a mounted break-out but, despite optimistic forecasts for the Battle of Arras, the cavalry was unable to be used in their

Silver statuette of a mounted officer, Royal Scots Greys. Presented to Captain H.B. Towse, Royal Scots Greys, by his brother officers on the occasion of his marriage, 19th April 1909. *Hallmark: London 1906-07 Maker: Goldsmiths' and Silversmiths' Company Ltd.*

mounted role, and instead provided detachments of dismounted officers and men for service in the trenches. Increased use of dismounted cavalry as machine-gunners was begun, and all machine-gun sections within the cavalry brigades were organised together into machine-gun squadrons. At the same time, each squadron received a Hotchkiss light machine-gun for each of its troops and one section from each troop was organised as a Hotchkiss section. The cavalry was being taught all about how to use the weapon which had emasculated it in its traditional role. During May and June the Greys fielded an entire dismounted battalion, three squadrons – each of 100 men – and served in the trenches at Guillemont Farm. While there, a body of Greys volunteers conducted a highly successful raid into the German trenches opposite, causing many casualties and gathering a great deal of useful intelligence material; two Military Crosses and eleven Military Medals were awarded for the bravery and intrepidity of the officers and men involved.

During the German offensive of March 1918 the Greys suffered from much the same chaos and disorganisation which resulted from the strength and impetus of the advance as did the rest of the armies. Although the offensive had been foreseen, no one had predicted just how overwhelming its strength would be: about four to one in the Germans' favour. The Regiment was split up, dismounted and very busy indeed, tearing about the line desperately trying to stem the advance, plug gaps in the defences and fall back in good order, all at the same time. As the strength of the last serious German offensive of the war petered out, so the Greys formed part of the inexorable advance north and east which resulted in the armistice in November 1918. The advance, when it happened in August 1918, was

Silver statuette of a mounted trooper in service dress, marching order.
Commemorating the service of the Royal Scots Greys in the 5th Cavalry
Brigade of the 2nd Cavalry Division, France, Belgium and Germany
1914-18. Presented to Lieut.-Colonel J.J. Readman DSO and Officers of
the Royal Scots Greys by Major J.G. Crabbe MC on his leaving the
Regiment October 1925. *Hallmark: London 1925-26. Maker:
Goldsmiths' and Silversmiths' Company Ltd.*

rapid and effective. It encountered little real opposition since Germany was
disintegrating internally, German morale was low and the will to continue the war
absent. At the end of October 1918 the Greys caught a whiff of the influenza
epidemic which was a precursor of that which was to sweep through Europe after
the armistice and kill more people than had the war, so that the Regiment was
immobilised and severely reduced in effective numbers.

The 5th Cavalry Brigade headed the march into Germany after the armistice,
the Greys having had a few days to smarten themselves up and send to York for
the guidon. The Brigade entered Belgium on 17 November and crossed the
border into Germany on 1 December, to occupy billets around the town of
Neudorf. After spending three weeks in Germany the Regiment returned to
Belgium and a type of normality. Life began again in the officers' and sergeants'
messes, a pack of hounds was organised and several race meetings held.
Demobilisation and requests for leave having taken their inevitable and rapid toll,
a much-depleted Regiment finally left Antwerp on 22 March 1919, bound for
Southampton. Its casualties during the war were 143 of all ranks killed or missing
and 446 wounded.

After being stationed for a year at home, at Redford Barracks in Edinburgh, the
Greys were warned for service overseas, the first time that the Regiment would
have served overseas in peacetime, and the ending of a tradition shared with the
Household Cavalry. At first service in India was foreseen, but service in Egypt
was the reality and, after a hectic round of equestrian events – the Sprot Cup
(regimental cross-country race), the Regimental Grey Horse Race, the
Regimental Point-to-Point and an outbreak of polo at Murrayfield – the

Regiment left from Southampton on 10 November 1920. Their grey horses, not able to be taken to Egypt, were handed over to the 1st (The King's) Dragoon Guards, who relieved them in Edinburgh, and the Greys arrived at Alexandria on 22 November.

Nationalist fervour in Egypt had only abated a little in the aftermath of the war, and a new and resurgent republican Turkey was making its presence felt in Near East politics. The Egypt posting was one fraught with possibilities for active service. Nothing major occurred in the year that the Greys spent in Egypt, however, except a tiring round of hunting, shooting and polo, and in November 1921 the Regiment moved to Palestine.

Palestine had been carved out of the territories of the old Turkish Empire and was being administered under mandate by the British, who did their best, a thankless task, to keep the Arabs from murdering the small quantities of Jewish settlers who were arriving from Europe. Raids on the Jewish settlements continued, however, despite the Regiment maintaining a squadron and two troops at short notice to move. The poor communications between the settlements and the garrison hindered the Regiment's effectiveness. Palestine offered much the same recreational opportunities for the Greys officers as had Egypt, to which the Regiment returned after six months in Palestine in May 1922. At the beginning of October the Regiment left Suez for India, arriving at Bombay on 17 October, the first time that the Royal Scots Greys had ever set hoof on the sub-continent. After a brief period in camp at Deolali the Regiment moved to Risalpur, where it relieved the 18th Hussars.

CHAPTER SEVEN

Amalgamation, Mechanisation and War

1923-1945

3rd Carabiniers

The amalgamated Regimental title was not adopted until 1928 although during the previous five years a number of halting, yet decreasingly uncomfortable, attempts were made to come to terms with the amalgamation. The marriage of the 3rd and 6th Dragoon Guards was achieved in late 1922 by disbanding C squadron of the 3rd and B and C squadrons of the Carabiniers and making the single squadron of Carabiniers the third squadron of the new Regiment.

Although in 1922 the British government had a list of precedents going back to the seventeenth century for raising and disbanding regiments as circumstances required, few amalgamations had been tried, and none had been applied in living memory to cavalry regiments. In 1881 the 109 regiments of line infantry had been chopped to a mere sixty-nine by widespread amalgamations. Allowing for the shrieks of protest which gradually died down (as protests usually do), these amalgamations were gradually, if grudgingly, accepted. The maintenance of separate identities between and within the separate battalions of infantry regiments had been allowed to continue, and even been encouraged in order to bolster the identity of the new infantry regiments after 1881. It is likely that this may have been the precedent employed when attempting to soften the blow which the cavalry amalgamations of 1922 represented to upholders of traditions in the regiments concerned.

A number of factors had to be borne in mind. The Regiment's title between 1922 and 1928 was "3rd/6th Dragoon Guards" – no soubriquet, sub-title or honorifics, merely an equal treatment of the former, if rather bald, titles. Both

Regimental standards were retained, the Carabinier one being carried by the third, or Carabiniers, squadron, when on parade. It might be thought that this dual-standard idea would lapse when one or other wore out or was due to be replaced, but this was not the case. In 1927 *two* new standards were presented by the Duke of Gloucester. Two sets of badges were worn, one by the first two squadrons, another by the Carabinier squadron, until 1929, although the whole Regiment wore the same shoulder title from 1922. There was the question of uniform too. Other ranks had not worn full dress uniform since 1914 and, with the principal exception of the bands, would no longer wear it. Officers retained it in theory until 1939, but it was most usually worn at Royal levées. While, in theory, no other ranks' uniform existed, a store had to be maintained for occasions when one or two, or even a guard of, soldiers would be needed to dress up. Prior to 1914 the 3rd Dragoon Guards' full dress uniform had been a scarlet tunic with yellow velvet collar and cuffs, dark blue overall trousers with a single broad yellow cloth seam stripe, a helmet with a black and red plume and belts of plain gold lace. The Carabiniers' uniform was all blue, with white cloth collar and cuffs on the tunic and double narrow white seam stripes on the overalls; their helmet plume was white and their pouch-belt still decorated with silver fittings. In mess dress, officers of the 3rd had worn a yellow waistcoat beneath their scarlet mess jackets; Carabiniers officers had a white waistcoat beneath a blue jacket. The years after the ending of the First World War were not prosperous ones, and the Army had both to adopt and to encourage economies. Therefore, no composite uniform was prescribed, but pieces of each of the old ones were utilised in combination. The resulting uniform was the 3rd's tunic with the Carabiniers' overalls, the Carabiniers' pouch-belt with the 3rd's helmet plume. The mess jacket of the 3rd was retained but worn with the Carabiniers' waistcoat and overalls. The new badges, first authorised in 1929, incorporated the most distinctive elements of both the old Regiments: crossed carbines behind the Prince of Wales' plumes, coronet and motto.

The amalgamated Regiment left India in 1924 and returned home to Colchester. In 1926, during 3rd Cavalry Brigade manoeuvres on Salisbury Plain, the Regiment appeared fully mounted for the last time, and in 1928, while stationed at Tidworth, its horse transport was replaced by various permutations of a motorised equivalent. At the same time that vehicles took over the job of transporting the Regiment's field supplies and necessaries, the internal organisation was changed. From three sabre squadrons it was reduced to two, with one squadron equipped and trained as a machine-gun squadron. Its strength was computed at the time as twenty-one officers, 458 other ranks and 277 horses. The machine-gun squadron was equipped with eight Vickers .303 medium, water-

Silver cup, the Machine-Gun Inter-Troop Challenge Cup, *now D Squadron Inter-Troop Gunnery Competition Trophy. Presented by Captain H.A. Grimshaw, 3/6 Dragoon Guards 1925. Hallmark: London 1923-24 Maker: Goldsmiths' and Silversmiths' Company Ltd.*

Silver cup, the Officers Jumping Challenge Cup. Presented to the Officers of the 3rd/6th Dragoon Guards by Lieut. B.R. Turner, August 1925. Hallmark: Sheffield 1924-25. Maker unidentified.

cooled machine-guns, two for each of the four troops. The mechanised transport consisted of six motor-cycles, three of which had sidecars, and eleven lorries.

For the next decade, in the face of persistently-imposed economies originally maintained by the Government's ten-year rule (that no war would be in fought in Europe for the next ten years, to be renewed annually until 1932), most arms of the Army experimented with different types of strategy and tactics based largely on the lessons of the First World War. That the tank was here to stay was not in question, but its method of use was constantly questioned, and the fate of the horse remained both undecided and a contentious issue. Armoured cars were far more socially and strategically acceptable than tanks – since they, like horses, could be used in India and the Near and Far East – and concepts of extra-European warfare dominated the arguments until 1934, when the national government realised that things were afoot in Germany. During manoeuvres in England in the 1920s and early 1930s constant comparisons were made between the relative merits of differing types of vehicle and the horse, vis-à-vis their suitability for contemporary warfare. Their usefulness for reconnaissance, for transport of – for instance – the machine-gun squadron, their speed across country and their relative degrees of economy were assessed. In some cases vehicles won, in others horses; in a few cases no conclusion seems to have been reached. First of the British cavalry to be mechanised were the 11th Hussars (Prince Albert's Own) and the 12th Lancers (Prince of Wales's), who exchanged horses for armoured cars in 1927. Not until a decade later was it decided to mechanise the remainder of the cavalry, and even then the Household Cavalry, the Greys and 1st (Royal) Dragoons escaped. In those intervening ten years the role of the unmechanised cavalry continued to be debated and experimented with, the 3rd Carabiniers losing half their machine-guns in 1930 and having their scouts and signallers transported in Austin motor-cars as a third sabre squadron was resurrected. The Regiment sailed for India in this form in 1936, to be quartered at the familiar station of Sialkot, and – a year later – received the news of impending mechanisation.

Conversion from horses to light tanks took fifteen months, from January 1938 to March 1939, and was achieved by the drafting in of instructors from the Royal Tank Corps, the successors of those who had operated the tanks on the Western Front in the First World War. The Corps had been a permanent part of the Army since 1923 and had effectively monopolised the tanks until the cavalry were mechanised. Six months after the Carabiniers had been declared fit to look after their own tanks, war was declared.

Although Germany's intentions were clear and those of Italy suspect, plans which Japan might be making in any specific direction were, although regarded suspiciously, far from certain in 1939. A force of some strength therefore had to remain in India to counter not only likely Japanese aggression but also, potentially, that of Russia. The Russo-German non-aggression pact of early 1939 had meant that, until the German invasion of Russia in 1941, Britain could not be sure that Russia would not launch a second front, on behalf of the Axis powers, into northern India. Therefore, although quantities of Indian infantry were dispatched to North Africa, to join forces already there intent upon defending Egypt and the Suez Canal from first Italian and then German aggression, the 1st Indian Armoured Division was not formed until a year after the outbreak of war. The Carabiniers were not mobilised until October 1941, two months prior to the outbreak of war with Japan.

On 1 February 1941 the Regiment had contributed eleven officers and 102 other ranks to the formation of a new unit, the 25th Dragoons. The Commanding Officer, Lieutenant-Colonel Spencer Horn MC, was a Carabinier who had been commissioned in the 3rd Dragoon Guards in October 1914. He subsequently relinquished command of the 25th Dragoons to return to command the 3rd Carabiniers, but the Regiment continued forming, equipping and training until it was ready for service in Burma at the end of 1943. After fighting throughout the Burma campaign, the 25th Dragoons was disbanded, having earned five battle honours, in June 1948.

In November 1941, while the Regiment was forming part of the 2nd Armoured Brigade of the 1st Indian Armoured Division, it received its first issue (three) of the new American light tanks – "Stuarts". These replaced the obsolete British type previously in service. They were mounted with a 37mm gun and three .30

4 cups.

Back: Silver. International Horse Show, Olympia, London 1936. First Prize for the Best Trained Riding Horse (Dressage Test). Presented by Mrs Claude F. Goddard. Awarded to 3rd Carabiniers. *Hallmark: Birmingham 1935-36. Maker: William Adams Ltd.*

Front, left: Electro-plated nickel silver. Royal Scots Greys Regimental Tennis Tournament 1932. *Awarded in 1961 and 1977 for mixed doubles.*

Front, centre: Silver. Colchester Garrison Rifle Competition, inter-unit Revolver Competition 1924. Won by 3/6 Dragoon Guards. *Hallmark: Birmingham 1923-24. Maker: S Blanckensee and Son Ltd*

Front, right: Silver. The Tenth Hussars Challenge Cup. Presented by Members Cpls. Mess X.R.H. to Cpls Mess 3rd Carabiniers, October 1935. For Annual Tennis (Singles) Championship.
Hallmark: Birmingham 1929-30. Maker unidentified.

Browning machine-guns and accommodated a crew of four within the turret and hull, the armour of which varied in thickness from 51mm to 10mm; the tanks' top speeds were thirty-six miles per hour – on good roads. The Stuart tanks, named after General J.E.B. Stuart, a Confederate cavalry general of great panache, supplemented the vehicles with which the Regiment had been equipped since relinquishing their British light tanks. Such were the exigencies of war, however, that the Regiment's organisation was changed from being of three squadrons of light tanks to two of medium and one of light tanks, and then changed again to being three of medium tanks. All very confusing.

By the end of May some sort of agreement had been reached and the Regiment's strength arranged as follows: three "Grant" tanks, seven "Lee" tanks and three "Stuart" tanks. Headquarters squadron was mounted in armoured carriers, their nicknames reflecting the degree of interest which remained in equestrianism: the Scout troop had the names of hounds, the Mortar troop those of race-courses, and those of Headquarters squadron itself were drawn straight from R.S. Surtees' hunting novels of the 1850s, one carrier sporting the name "Mr Sponge". The names "Grant" and "Lee" were British soubriquets for the two marques of tank that the Americans, who made them and supplied them under the lend-lease agreement, called the M3. Both versions mounted two principal guns, a 37mm gun in the turret (therefore capable of traversing through 360 degrees), and a 75mm gun mounted in a sponson on the right side of the hull and restricted to traversing through thirty degrees. Acquisition of the Grant gave the British, for the first time, a tank that had superior fire power to any German tank of the period and, accommodating a crew of six, both the Grant and the Lee (named after opposing generals of the War between the States) were comparatively roomy inside. The advantage of the 75mm sponson-mounted gun was that it could fire both armour-piercing and high-explosive ammunition at will, this capability not being afforded by the 37mm turret-mounted gun. Essential differences between the marques of M3 supplied to the Carabiniers under the names of Grant and Lee were that the Grant had a turret which overhung at the rear, in which the wireless equipment was housed, and did not have an armoured cupola, mounting a .30 Browning machine-gun, on its turret; the earlier versions of the Lee had riveted, not cast, hulls, but this ill-advised idea was dropped on later editions.

The arrival of their small quantity of tanks had no sooner tantalised the Regiment with an implicit likelihood of active service than they were whisked away in June and July 1942 to the Middle East where, it was felt, they could be put to better use. Defeat of the *Afrika Korps* in the Western Desert seemed likely, that of Japan in Burma seemed rather far away, and it was a case of utilising limited resources where they could do most good. The Carabiniers were left without any tanks at at all and appear to have been rather at a loss as regards what was intended for them. In September 1942 Major Ralph Younger MC, 7th Hussars, became second-in-command, succeeding to command between 1943 and 1944. He commanded the Greys from 1947 to 1948, retired as a Major General with a fistful of decorations in 1958, and was Colonel of the Royal Scots Dragoon Guards from 1971 until 1974.

By February 1943 some more Grant and Lee tanks arrived, as did more Stuarts, but by July only the Stuarts were left; shortly afterwards these too were withdrawn and Lees were substituted. By this time, as a previous regimental historian, Colonel Oatts, has wryly observed, the Regiment could drive just about anything. During the previous year the Regiment's Brigade had been renumbered 251st Indian Armoured Brigade, within the renumbered 31st Indian Armoured Division, but in October 1943 this brigade was disbanded and the Regiment made an independent unit, incorporating a workshop section, an ordnance field park section, a light aid detachment and a tank recovery section. Prospects of active service loomed and enthusiasm overrode cynicism. Despite removal of the field park section, the Regiment moved to the India-Burma frontier in December 1943 and prepared itself for action. It formed part of 254th

3 boxing belts, 3rd Carabiniers 1936.
Top: Light Weight, Middle: Welter Weight,
Bottom: Middle Weight (the Hume Belt, presented by Mrs
A. du P.T. Cole). Awarded 1936-40, 1956-59, 1965-67. N.
R. Haines won the Welter Weight belt as a Lance-Corporal
in 1937, as a Corporal in 1938 and as a Sergeant in 1939/40.
Hallmark: Chester and Birmingham 1935-36. Maker
unidentified.

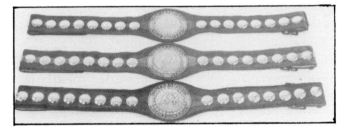

Silver cup, the Cavalry Football Association Challenge Cup 1934-35. Won by 3rd Carabiniers (Saddler-Corporal A Robinson gaining two hat-tricks). Hallmark: London 1934-35. Maker: Henry Phillips.

Indian Tank Brigade and was located at Imphal.

Burma was not seen as tank country; there were no wide, dry plains where armoured units could indulge in uninterrupted sweeps of terrain. The Burma campaign was not one of swift movement by conventional forces, although the unconventional Japanese had succeeded in scything through it fairly rapidly, and retaking Burma was – it was recognised – going to be an arduous and rather disagreeable business. Tanks were envisaged as being used in the close support role to infantry, as mobile fire platforms and as a means of bolstering and transporting foot-soldiers. To learn this role, the Regiment began training with 1st Battalion the Seaforth Highlanders.

The Japanese were, not unnaturally, aware of British intentions at Imphal, and moved forward to combat them from Burma. Both sides engaged in a series of almost hesitant reconnaissance patrols, in varying degrees of strength, and not until 26 March 1944 were the Carabiniers committed by one of these to serious action. In a short and heated action following an ambush at Nanmaw, five miles south of Tamu, two troops of the Regiment – commanded by Major A.J. Pettit – took out five Japanese tanks and captured a sixth, which was eventually put back into working order and sent as a present to the Commander of the 14th Army,

General Sir William Slim. Only one of Pettit's tanks was seriously hit, and he sustained six casualties in the course of the brief, if frantic, action.

The Japanese forces attacked in March and attempted to encircle the 17th Indian Division at Imphal. British forces there, including the 3rd Carabiniers, withdrew into a series of defensive "boxes". The Regiment was largely split up by squadron and troop, both at Imphal and elsewhere, and consequently divided between defensive boxes and training areas. The whole of IV Corps, of which the division formed a part, was soon surrounded, but Allied air superiority meant not only that it could be supported from the air, but also that it could be reinforced from the same direction. This was an advantage denied to the Japanese, whose lines of communication and supply were both dangerously extended and increasingly weakened. At the end of April 1944 British forces broke out of their defensive positions and began to counter-attack. A squadron of the Regiment was soon in action at Ningthookong, in support of 1st Battalion 4th Gurkha Rifles, but received severe damage in the process and had to withdraw; the position was finally taken by tanks and Gurkhas at the end of the month.

Earlier in April B squadron had been in action in support of 3rd Battalion 9th Jat Regiment in assaulting a position at Nunshigum, north of Imphal. The Nunshigum ridge was a precipitous one and the Japanese so well entrenched that the attack on 11 April had to be abandoned. Because of the impervious nature of the Japanese bunkers to both air attack and long-range artillery fire, it was decided that, for the renewed attack, the infantry, 1st Dogras, would have to be closely supported by the Carabiniers' tanks. This meant taking tanks up very steep inclines and through terrain which would severely reduce their speed and mobility and, in consequence, make them very vulnerable. The attack began on 13 April. The first summit was reached quickly enough, but then the tanks had to proceed in line, flanked by the infantry, at a slow pace and with the tank commanders unable to close their turret hatches because of their need both to see what was happening and to communicate quickly with the infantry. Once the supporting air and artillery barrage ceased, the Japanese attacked the tanks on foot, causing heavy casualties among the commanders and their replacements. Forward movement largely ceased as, one by one, the tanks' crews were put out of action by accurate Japanese shooting. Displaying commendable initiative, and acting on Colonel Younger's orders (which were still coming through on the tanks' wireless sets), Squadron Sergeant-Major Craddock, in allegiance with Subadar Ranbir Singh of the Dogras, outflanked the Japanese positions and, by drawing and returning their fire with the few tanks left operational, if only by their drivers, distracted them in order that the Dogras could advance and take out their positions. Craddock was awarded the Distinguished Conduct Medal and

Tanks of the 3rd Carabiniers in Burma, 1944-45. Presented to the Regiment in memory of Brigadier F J S Whetstone OBE, who commanded it from 1944 to 1946 and again from 1948 to 1950. Artist: Frank Wootton (1911-)

two other soldiers received Military Medals; Ranbir Singh was awarded the Indian Order of Merit.

The tanks of C squadron were engaged on a number of occasions during the rest of the Battle of Imphal, principally in support of infantry under the most dangerous and trying conditions. After leave, and action in the Chin Hills, the Regiment was ready to participate in the full assault into Burma at the beginning of November 1944. In December the River Chindwin was crossed on rafts and B squadron operated with a company of the Royal Berkshire Regiment in dense jungle, sustaining several casualties among their senior officers from Japanese snipers. As the British advanced south, so the Japanese withdrew before them, rarely contesting much ground, and the speed of the invasion grew. B squadron continued to pursue the enemy, moving without the aid of tank transporters, so difficult was the terrain, and the River Irrawaddy was reached and crossed at the end of February 1945. The various squadrons of the Carabiniers were placed in support of different infantry columns and, again, operated largely separately. Rangoon was reached by the Regiment on 28 May, after several bloody engagements, and the Carabiniers sailed for India on 18 June 1945, moving to Ahmednagar shortly after arrival. Casualties during the fourteen months between March 1944 and May 1945 were eighty-two, all ranks, killed, and 147, all ranks, wounded. The Regiment was to remain in India until 1946.

Royal Scots Greys

The Greys remained in Risalpur until 1925, getting back up to strength, training for the possibilities of service on the frontier, enjoying the benefits of service in India and indulging in as much polo, hunting, shooting and riding as possible. Participation in horse shows increased and was encouraged, and Squadron Sergeant-Major Frier won cups at two shows in 1924. Hockey became a regimental game, played during the summer months in the hill station of Khanspur in the Muree Hills. In 1925 the Regiment moved to Meerut to relieve the 11th Hussars, marching 610 miles south-east along the Grand Trunk Road, taking two months and doing the journey in forty-eight stages. While in Meerut in 1925 the Regiment took part in several horse shows (where the musical ride was much in demand and where Squadron Sergeant-Major Frier repeated his triumph at Risalpur), brought its polo team to become one of the best in the Army, won a couple of steeplechases and took part in pig-sticking competitions. The following year the Regimental boxing team won the All-India Cavalry Boxing Cup for the third time, but in 1927 all this strenuous recreational self-indulgence was overshadowed by an impending return home.

The Regiment left India on 28 October and arrived at Southampton on 18 November, getting to Redford Barracks in Edinburgh on the following day. The grey horses which they had so reluctantly left in Edinburgh in 1920 were returned to them and were to be of considerable use in carrying out the Regiment's public duties for the next decade. One of the first of those duties was to accompany and guard the coffin of Field Marshal Lord Haig, who died in 1928; his son was to serve as an officer in the Regiment from 1938 to 1946. After a hectic social and recreational round throughout 1928, with a little training at the annual month's camp at Stobs, the Greys moved to Tidworth in 1929.

The Greys remained in Tidworth for the next four years, largely unaffected by murmurings about mechanisation, although concessions were made in the shape of a troop of Austin 7 motor-cars as a mechanised signal troop. Tattoos, horse shows, polo tournaments, race meetings and other sports and games seem to have occupied much of the large amount of organised leisure enjoyed by the Regiment, but some time was spent at annual camp. The Greys had, by the early 1930s, developed a powerful reputation for the strength of their polo team and won the Subalterns' Cup in 1931, 1932 and 1934, being aided greatly by the presence in the Regiment of Humphrey Guinness, who played for the national team. In 1933 the Regiment returned to Edinburgh.

It had become the practice to spend June and July each year at camp and under

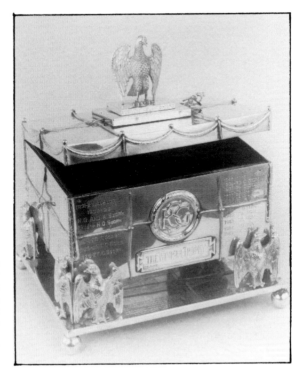

Silver model of a Red Cross parcel, the Winram Trophy.
Presented by the "Fund for British Soldiers interned in Germany", of which Mrs James Winram was Organiser and Honorary Secretary, to the Regiment of the Royal Scots Greys, Edinburgh 1920. To be competed for annually by the Non- Commissioned Officers and Men of the Royal Scots Greys and to be awarded to the squadron gaining the highest number of points in Sports Competition, as decided by the Officers of the Regiment. *Hallmark: Edinburgh 1920-21. Maker: Hamilton and Inches*

canvas in order to teach recruits about, and remind old sweats of, active service conditions. In 1934, however, the Commanding Officer – Lieutenant-Colonel George Pigot Moodie – decided that it was time that the Regiment made its presence known through Scotland to those Scots who might, under the influence of infantry propaganda, have believed that all Scottish regiments were foot-soldiers. The Regiment had recruited solely from Scotland for some time, but was in competition for recruits with Highland and Lowland regiments which had specific recruiting areas of the country allocated to them. Colonel Pigot Moodie managed to persuade the Army's authorities to allow him to take a mounted party of the Regiment, himself and twenty other officers, 250 other ranks and 200 horses, on a tour of Scotland to "show the flag". The march took twenty-three days and covered 470 miles. Hospitality abounded all the way, and what would now be called the "publicity value" of the march was considerable, despite the generally poor weather. The number of recruits increased during the year in question by approximately a third, and during the march several opportunities were taken to train; in exercises with aircraft, in reconnaissance and in river crossings.

For the greater part of 1935 the round of training and recreation continued in

Scotland, the Regiment actively participating in ceremonies connected with King George V's Silver Jubilee. In November 1935 the Greys left Scotland and moved to Aldershot, where they joined the 1st Cavalry Brigade. In 1937 the grave of Ensign Charles Ewart was discovered in a disused cemetery in Manchester and the remains were disinterred, to be reburied in 1938 in a tomb on the esplanade of Edinburgh Castle. Another discovery of similar significance was that the perceived threat of mechanisation was again hanging over the Regiment's head. In an effort to alert Scotland to this radical and regimentally unpopular idea, the Commanding Officer brought it to the attention of each of the Scottish Members of Parliament, in the hope of enlisting their hope to resist it. The press also grasped the story and did their best to fan public opinion in order to prevent mechanisation. How much the War Office's actions owed to the public outcry, how much to the influence of the Scottish MPs and how much to other reasons is not recorded, but the Greys were not mechanised. Lieutenant-Colonel Cyril Gaisford St Lawrence, however, received a strongly-worded reprimand from the Army Council for the unorthodox way in which he had seen fit to criticise Army policy.

In October 1937 the Regiment moved to Hounslow, played a lot of polo, took part in manoeuvres near Basingstoke in August 1938, and on 10 September was told that it was to move at very short notice to Palestine. Two squadrons and the machine-gun troop, plus Regimental headquarters, were to go; C squadron was to return to Edinburgh to form the beginnings of a mounted depot. At the end of the month, taking their horses, they left Britain and arrived at Haifa ten days later.

The Regiment's function in Palestine was similar to that exercised by them seventeen years previously, in 1921; keeping the Jewish settlers and the Arabs apart. Dawn raids on suspected Arab villages were the norm, rarely producing much in the way of illegal caches of arms, but the mounted Regiment was capable to a far greater degree of the silent surprise approach to such villages than a motorised column would have been. Its role was in direct support of the Palestine Police Force, and it was stationed for eighteen months at Rehovot, fifteen miles from Jaffa. In January 1939 it spent three weeks on manoeuvres with the Trans-Jordan Frontier Force and a selection of British regiments in the Jordan valley.

On the outbreak of war in September 1939 the mounted depot in Edinburgh was the point to which all the Regiment's reservists had to report. Several hundred of them having reported, many of whom were no doubt looking forward to being mounted again, they were all promptly posted to a labour battalion in France, where it was probably felt they were needed far more than in Palestine. The remaining cavalry reservists, officers and other ranks, joined the Regiment in Palestine by the middle of October 1939.

Palestine remained relatively unaffected by the opening moves of the war and,

Lieutenant-Colonel G C T Keyes VC, MC, Croix de Guerre (1917-1941).
Born in Aberdour, Fife, Keyes was the son of Admiral of the Fleet Lord Keyes. He joined the Royal Scots Greys in 1937. He volunteered for the Commandos and raised a troop of 11th (Scottish) Commando in 1940, going with them to the Middle East in 1941. He won his Military Cross in Syria in 1941 and his posthumous Victoria Cross after being killed during an attack on the desert headquarters of Lieutenant-General, later Field Marshal, Erwin Rommel, commander of the Afrika Korps. Artist: Sydney P Kendrick (1874-1955).

Silver model of a Vickers .303 medium machine-gun, the Dugdale Trophy. Presented by Capt. T.L. Dugdale (Royal Scots Greys), 1925 for inter-team machine-gun competition. Hallmark: London 1925-26. Maker: Goldsmiths' and Silversmiths' Company Ltd.

despite occasional outbursts, the need for the Regiment to remain constantly alert in order to deal with terrorists decreased. Although the Middle East remained something of a backwater until Italy entered the war, the Regiment continued its equestrian training in the hope of being employed in some capacity. Its lack of mechanisation, especially once the campaigns in Libya, Abyssinia and Eritrea began, meant that it could not be considered for active service, and so it continued to send officers and men away on detached duty to other units. Most notable among these were Lieutenants Michael Borwick, Geoffrey Keyes and William McLean, all of whom left the Regiment to join the newly forming, and glamorously mysterious, commandos. Although Borwick was to be captured on Crete, Keyes and McLean both became lieutenant-colonels rapidly, while still in their early twenties, and were highly decorated. McLean won two Distinguished Service Orders for intrepidity in Yugoslavia, and Keyes acquired a Military Cross prior to the posthumous award of a Victoria Cross for an attack by his commandos on Rommel's headquarters.

The early years of the war were characterised in the British Army by the existence of short-lived military forces and columns, the titles of which were drawn from their commanders' surnames. The resulting wide variety of martial-sounding unit titles thus so originally achieved has been satirized by Evelyn Waugh in his novels about the war. A survey of the Greys' activities in 1940 and 1941 reveals first *Bluecol*, then *Trotcol*, *Heyforce* and *Habforce* and finally *Todcol*. Of all these forces, only *Bluecol* departed from convention inasmuch as it took its title from the nickname, 'Bluebell', of Lieutenant D.N. Stewart. The nickname resulted from that officer's habitually highly-polished appearance, due – it was implied – to lavish use of a metal polish called Bluebell. *Todcol*, named after the Regiment's commanding officer, Lieutenant-Colonel G.H.N. Todd, was formed in May 1941 to take part in the invasion of Syria. The column consisted of Regimental Headquarters, the machine-gun troop and A squadron, with B squadron of the Staffordshire Yeomanry, and initially formed part of the reserve of the invasion force, being added to the 7th Australian Division. Syria was held in some strength by Vichy French forces and initial progress was slow. On the 11th June *Todcol* was reinforced by Australian light tanks, infantry, and anti-tank and anti-aircraft guns and ordered forward in support of other Australian forces towards Merj Ayoun. After a hard-fought advance against numerically superior French forces, the hastily-formed brigade was fiercely counter-attacked on the 15th June and forced to withdraw from its broad front, in some confusion and after sustaining losses. After a series of counter-attacks by both sides, the French eventually withdrew from Merj Ayoun in the face of growing British, Indian, Australian and Free French forces. *Todcol*, the formation of which had necessitated rapid and partial mechanisation – into motor lorries, was disbanded in August 1941. Its existence, and the experience of mechanisation thus provided, proved valuable to the Regiment, which was gradually coming to terms with its new role and the inevitable battlefield obsolescence of the horse.

That mechanisation was on the way was not doubted, and rumours to that effect became fact in May 1941 when the announcement arrived that the Greys were to be mechanised. The Regiment's first tanks, on which conversion was practised, were Stuarts, the same type as those given to the 3rd Carabiniers in India and popularly nicknamed "Honeys". Adaptation came comparatively quickly and, in February 1942, the Greys moved close to Cairo to form part of 8th Armoured Brigade within 10th Armoured Division.

For the next three months, having learnt how to control their tanks, the Regiment was taught how to use them in the rapidly-developing concept of desert-based armoured warfare. In April 1942 the first Grant tanks arrived for the Greys, and these supplemented the main Regimental strength of Stuarts. After the fall of Tobruk on 20 June the 8th Army withdrew, the Greys being part of the retreat, and the Regiment relinquished its tanks; the Stuarts to 4th County of

London Yeomanry, the Grants to the Tank Delivery Regiment. By 8 June, however, re-equipped with Stuarts, Grants and Lees, the Greys were back in Mareopolis, twenty miles south of Alexandria.

At the end of August the Regiment became involved in its first tank battle, when the *Afrika Korps* made its advance towards the Nile Delta and Cairo. Moving to the support of other outnumbered armoured regiments, the Greys gained valuable experience in action for the loss of two Grant tanks. At the Battle of El Alamein in September 1942 the Regiment formed part of 7th Armoured Division, and were with the force which was shelled while being caught between two minefields. Eventually escaping from that trap, the Greys moved forward as the German forces retreated towards Tripoli.

In November 1942, during the advance on Tripoli, the Regiment formed the right echelon of the 4th Light Armoured Brigade and was bowling along, minding its own business, when a battery of Italian guns were unwise enough to draw attention to their presence by opening fire. The two heavy squadrons, in Grants, returned fire at long range with their 75mm sponson-mounted guns, while the light squadron, in Stuarts, worked round to a flank. The squadron leader, Major Frank Bowlby, interpreting the Commanding Officer's order to attack from the flank in true cavalry spirit, led his Stuarts in a bumping, bounding charge with all guns firing. B squadron overran the battery, persuaded them of the error of their ways in a kind, but occasionally terminal, manner, and secured eleven guns, thirty vehicles and 300 prisoners at the cost of one tank lost and no casualties to the Regiment.

In mid-November, during the westward advance on Tripoli, having gradually lost tanks during the few small engagements in which it was involved, and others due to mechanical difficulties, the Regiment obtained new tanks from a squadron of the Warwickshire Yeomanry. Included among these were two "Shermans", the tank that the Americans called the M4 and which was to characterise much of the Allied armour for the remainder of the war. Although mounting only one gun, in its turret, the Sherman's gun was of 75mm calibre, the same as the sponson-mounted gun in the Grant and Lee tanks, and its armour was a considerable improvement over that of its predecessors: 75mm in the turret, 50mm in the hull. With its crew of five it was less roomy than either the Grant or the Lee, but it gave those who used it an advantage, briefly, over the opposing German tanks. Its armament was completed by two .30 Browning machine-guns mounted in turret and hull, and one .50 Browning mounted on top of the turret and intended as an anti-aircraft weapon.

By the end of November 1942 the Regiment had relinquished most of its tanks to other units, but then took over those of 1st Royal Tank Regiment, most of which were Shermans. By 12 December its strength in tanks was: Regimental Headquarters, three Stuarts and one Grant; A squadron, one Stuart, two Grants and six Shermans; B squadron, sixteen Stuarts; C squadron, one Stuart, one Grant and eleven Shermans. This was the force which the Regiment took in the advance from El Agheila, on the Gulf of Sirte, beyond which they finally caught up with the retreating German rearguard. A brief action followed, the Germans losing the heat by two tanks to one. On 17 December, at Nofilia, contact was resumed with the *Afrika Korps* and the Regiment was ordered to engage the enemy by General Freyberg, commanding the New Zealand Division.

The Commanding Officer, Lieutenant-Colonel Sir Ranulph Twisleton-Wykeham-Fiennes (known for reasons principally of shorthand as "Lugs"), led the attack mounted in his command vehicle, a Stuart with the turret removed, known as *Astra*. A rapid attack on the flank of the German position led them into its centre and a considerable fire-fight resulted, the rapidity of the Greys' charge introducing a large element of surprise and catching many of the enemy, including two anti-tank batteries, completely unprepared. The Germans counter-attacked from positions that the Regiment had not reached, and a duel took place for the remainder of the day, the Greys losing seven tanks and an officer and two men.

More fighting occurred all the way to Tripoli, which was occupied before the end of January 1943, and the Regiment settled for a period of rest and retraining in and around Tripoli. For a brief period, B squadron seemed about to convert from their light Stuart tanks to British Crusaders – a marque virtually obsolete by that time – but in the event the Regiment's strength was fixed at three squadrons of Shermans.

The Greys' next action was at Salerno, south of Naples on the Italian mainland. The Regiment's squadrons were separated for training and for the landing; A squadron joining 167th Infantry Brigade, B squadron 201st Guards Brigade and C squadron 169th Infantry Brigade. The Regiment left Tripoli on 4 September 1943 and the landing-craft and assault ships arrived off Salerno on 9 September. A and C squadrons landed with the first wave and were quickly in action against a well-entrenched and highly-motivated German defence. Some delay in providing the much-needed support for the beleaguered infantry was caused by boggy ground, in which eight tanks stuck temporarily, but they were freed in time to engage German tanks which were seriously impeding the infantry's advance. Sergeant McMeekin took out four tanks in rapid succession, A squadron having attacked and surprised them in the flank, and later received the Military Medal for his good shooting. The Battle of Salerno continued until 16 September, with the Allied forces gradually gaining ground, linking with the 8th Army, who had

An incident during the fighting around Caen, Normandy, 1944. Destruction of farms and fences had left many loose horses in the Normandy countryside; this picture depicts a brief return to the joys of riding by troopers of the Royal Scots Greys during a lull in the fighting. Watercolour. Artist: Oliphant (dates unknown)

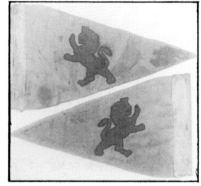

Pennants flown on the converted "Stuart" tank Astra *of the Commanding Officer of the Royal Scots Greys, Lieutenant-Colonel Sir Ranulph Twisleton-Wykeham-Fiennes, Bart. from El Alamein to Nofilia, where the tank was knocked out. The pennants are versions of the Royal Arms of Scotland, the Commanding Officer of the Greys being allowed dispensation to fly them from his tank.*

advanced up Italy from Sicily, and with the Regiment united again. Naples was entered on 1 October and the Regiment advanced with the rest of the Allied forces pushing up the west side of the Italian peninsula. The country was far from ideal for tanks, and tactically the advance up into Italy was a frustrating experience for the armour. The Regiment was withdrawn from the line in December 1943, returned to Naples and, handing over their tanks to 50th Royal Tank Regiment, left Naples at the end of January for Britain.

The invasion of north-west Europe was being planned, and when the Greys returned to Scotland on 9 February, moving at once to Worthing in Sussex the following day, it was clear that the Regiment was going to be a part of it. New tanks were received, Sherman Mk IIs, not as popular as the diesel Sherman IIIs which the Regiment had driven in Italy, with one Sherman Vc allocated to each troop. The Mk Vc Sherman mounted a seventeen-pounder gun and was the most powerfully armed British tank of the war; known as the Firefly, it was equal in armament to the latest marques of German tanks and was to prove a valuable asset in the assault on France. As a mobile gun platform par excellence, its crew was reduced to four, the hull machine-gunner (and his gun) being removed to maximise ammunition storage.

The Regiment formed part of 4th Armoured Brigade and landed between 7 and 9 June on the beaches north of Caen. Their operational role between the landing and the middle of August was to form the left of the British 2nd Army, which had landed on "Sword", "Juno" and "Gold" beaches on 6 June and which formed the left of the Allied invasion force. The object of the exercise was to draw off the predictably fierce German resistance into and around the Caen sector, allowing the American 1st Army, which had landed on "Omaha" and "Utah" beaches, to pivot around it, break out on the right and race for Paris. Gradually the British position around Caen grew stronger, necessitating the withdrawal of opposing German armour from other sectors, and the Regiment was heavily involved in engaging German tanks, usually of the superior Tiger or Panther types, around Caen to the west and south.

At Hill 112, south-west of Caen, between the Rivers Odon and Orne, in early July 1944, the Regiment's advance to support the infantry was dependent upon overlooking high ground being cleared before so many tanks could be risked in such an open salient. German tanks were so positioned, with their guns ranged-in accurately on a particular ridge, that they could hit any British tank which appeared over it on the only track available. The terrain – rolling country with woods and hedges – made it ideal for armour to fight defensive actions in, but difficult to fight offensive ones. So, until the weight of numbers told, the Germans were able to delay the British advance considerably and inflict many casualties on the Regiment, which got its own back occasionally – the eagle eye of Sergeant McMeekin being credited with the destruction of three out of six self-propelled guns and a tank in fairly quick succession. Caen fell on 13 July, and the Regiment was part of the Allied forces which advanced south to Falaise in time to inflict heavy casualties on the retreating German forces escaping through the gap between Allied forces south of the town. The action at Falaise effectively ended German resistance in that area of Normandy and, from then on, the Regiment headed east in pursuit of the retreating German armies.

Compared to the eleven weeks of intense fighting in Normandy, the speed of the Regiment's advance east to the Low Countries was remarkable. Leaving the Falaise area on 24 August the Greys were in Belgium by 5 September and, after encountering some resistance north of Brussels, were in the Netherlands before the end of the month. During the winter of 1944 the type of fighting which developed on the Dutch-German border did not involve the Greys, and they did not go into action again until the end of February 1945 when, for a week, they and accompanying forces fought their way into Germany and through the Hochwald to open the road to the Rhine.

By the end of April the Rhine had been taken, one squadron had crossed the Elbe and the Allied vice was closing on Germany. The eastern jaw of the vice was represented by the forces of the Russian Army, already perceived by Westminster, and possibly by Washington, as the next potential enemy. Aware that what the Russians took they were likely to keep, if only for bargaining purposes, it rapidly became apparent that some means had to be found of denying them the Danish peninsula and archipelago, and so a combined force of the Regiment and the 1st Canadian Parachute Regiment was sent on an eastward dash to seal off Denmark from the advancing Russians. The Regiment's tanks left Luneberg on 1 May; C squadron, which had already crossed the Elbe, was leading, carrying the Canadians on the back of the tanks, speeding along roads crowded with German refugees fleeing west from the Russians. They reached Wismar on the Baltic at one o'clock in the afternoon of 2 May. The vanguard of the Russian Army arrived eight hours later and did their best to seem pleased to see the Greys and the Canadians.

The Regiment began a seven-year posting in Germany from Wismar in 1945, and as soon as one war ended and a far colder one began, commenced the new role now so familiar to them.

CHAPTER EIGHT
Eagle and Carbine

1946-1988

3rd Carabiniers

The Regiment was to remain in India until 1946. It returned to a Europe greatly changed, torn by the ravages of the war and very different to the continent from which the Carabiniers had sailed ten years before. India had been left with some relief, as the sub-continent lurched bloodily towards partition, but returning home meant coming to terms with a new set of values, a different kind of society and a new sort of threat to national stability.

Britain was two years into the term of office of the Labour Government of Clement Attlee when the Carabiniers came back; a government that was trying to run a country virtually bankrupted by the war, with overseas responsibilities diminished only by the loss of India, and one committed to a radical programme of welfare and nationalisation. America had the Bomb, Russia had the greater part of eastern Europe, and Britain had debts, a far-flung empire which was becoming increasingly tiresome in places, and an Army that it could not afford to maintain. All the demobilisations of wartime soldiers had been completed by 1947, but National Service continued. The talk was of reductions, amalgamations and even disbandments. The disappearance of the Indian Army in 1948 involved the transfer of many officers from that service to the British Army, and this temporary enlargement made sweeping reductions even more likely. However, the Russian siege of Berlin in 1948, the daily worsening situation in what shortly became Israel, and increasing terrorist activity in Malaya all combined to stave off the dreaded Army cuts. The outbreak of the Korean War, following shortly after the Communist takeover in China, contrived to convince the government that its defence capability was not yet ripe for reduction.

During the Korean War of 1950-53 the Regiment contributed some soldiers to the first British armoured unit to go to Korea, 8th (King's Royal Irish) Hussars, who served in Korea from November 1950 until December 1951, when they were relieved by 5th Royal Inniskilling Dragoon Guards. The British forces in Korea were allied for the purposes of organisation with other Commonwealth units after July 1951, and the British armoured presence was successively accompanied by C, B and A squadrons of Lord Strathcona's Horse (Royal Canadians 2nd Armoured Regiment). Other than C squadron 7th Royal Tank Regiment and 1st and 5th Royal Tank Regiments, no other Commonwealth armoured units served in Korea.

Three of the volunteers from the Carabiniers who joined the 8th Hussars at the beginning of the war, as did volunteers of all ranks from other units of the Royal Armoured Corps, were killed during it.

Unlike C squadron, 7th Royal Tank Regiment, who had to make do with "Crocodiles", flame-throwing tanks based on the Churchill tank used at the end of World War II, the 8th Hussars were equipped with the latest marque of British tank, the Centurion Mk III. The 8th had three sabre squadrons of Centurions and a reconnaissance troop of elderly Cromwell Mk IIIs. The Centurions performed very efficiently during the Korean War, suffering few mechanical deficiencies or breakdowns, and their twenty-pounder main armament made them formidable opposition for the weakly-tanked Chinese. Ironically, the first shot to be fired in anger by a Centurion, fired by *Caughoo* of C squadron, 8th Hussars, on 11 February 1951, was fired against a British tank. This was no thinly-disguised attempt at a statement of Irish nationalism, however, but in response to a captured Cromwell which had unwisely attempted to engage C squadron with 75mm high explosive, quite ineffectively. The second shot from *Caughoo*, commanded by Captain George Strachan, silenced the captured tank.

Five days later Captain Cottle, of C squadron, provided fire support so accurate for a battalion attack on Hill 327 by the Gloucestershire Regiment that the action became nicknamed Operation Copybook: bunker after bunker of entrenched Chinese were dispatched with pinpoint accuracy by the tank's gunner while the 8th's Commanding Officer, C squadron leader and his second-in-command sat in the turret and ate bacon and eggs.

Korea was an admirable testing-ground for the Centurion, the tank which was to equip the Royal Armoured Corps until well into the 1960s (and foreign armies long after that). It provided only two major drawbacks: the terrain and the climate tended to allow the tanks to get bogged down easily – especially in the paddy-field ditches – and, if parked in mud on a winter's evening, the tanks would often become frozen too hard to the ground to move by the following morning. There

Silver cup and cover. Presented to the 3rd Carabiniers with grateful appreciation from the East Riding Yeomanry 1956. Hallmark: London 1896-97. Maker: Edward Barnard and Sons.

Silver statuette. 3rd Carabiniers (Prince of Wales's Dragoon Guards) Inter-Squadron Drill Competition Trophy. *Awarded 1955-1974. Hallmark: London 1955-56. Maker: Goodwood and Company Ltd*

were also panics at the beginning of the campaign about the new, and supposedly secret, tanks falling into enemy hands if abandoned and so, in the early months of the war, Centurions tended to be brought out of action sooner rather than later and, if necessary, blown up when abandoned. After a while, though, some unavoidably-abandoned tanks having been recovered, it was found that the only items removed from the interiors had been the ammunition – which was usually buried somewhere close by – and the pin-ups stuck inside by the crews.

After the Battle of the Imjin River, at which tanks of the 8th Hussars engaged swarm after swarm of Chinese, probably running down more than were machine-gunned, the Centurions' armament was supplemented. A .30 calibre Browning machine-gun was mounted on a ring around the commanders' hatches; this arrangement closely resembled the Scarff ring on which aircraft-mounted Lewis machine-guns had been fixed during the First World War.

Those Carabiniers who returned to the Regiment from their experiences in Korea would, one imagines, have been quite insufferable, not only about those experiences, but also about the wonders of the new Centurion tanks. Before long, though, the Regiment was driving Centurions in its role as one of the units of the British Army of the Rhine (BAOR), a role to which it, like all the regiments of the Royal Armoured Corps, soon became accustomed. Operations in Malaya, Brunei, against the Mau Mau in Kenya, or even in Suez in 1956, did not involve the Carabiniers, neither did the active side of the peace-keeping operations which went on sporadically in Cyprus from 1954.

The cavalry amalgamations of the late 1950s did not affect the Carabiniers because, it was stoutly maintained, they had already been amalgamated, thirty-five years before. Fortunately for the Army, if not necessarily for the cavalry, the implementation of the Government's defence limitation plan of 1957 was in the hands of a distinguished former infantry soldier who could be relied upon to appreciate the value of traditions and precedents but not let them get in his way: Field Marshal Sir Gerald Templer. The plan was envisaged as operating in several gradual stages, all of which would be spread over the following decade – so confident was the Conservative Government of Harold Macmillan of remaining in office for that length of time. National Service would be phased out, to end in 1961, overseas commitments would be cut, and amalgamations must take place. Accordingly, from 1958 to 1960, four new cavalry regiments were created from a former eight: The Queen's Dragoon Guards, The Queen's Own Hussars, The Queen's Royal Irish Hussars and the 9th/12th Royal Lancers. Templer succeeded relatively easily with the cavalry who, it might be thought, preferred amalgamations to disbandment (or marriage to death), and who were more adaptable than the Colonels of two Scottish infantry regiments who had to be induced to resign before their regiments could amicably form The Royal Highland Fusiliers.

In 1961 one of many incidents occurred in Britain's remaining sphere of influence in the Middle East which might, during the nineteenth century, have merited the description of "gunboat diplomacy". In view of its protection of British interests, together with those of a minor power dependent upon Britain (but on whose oil Britain was also dependent), it is safe to assume that Lord Palmerston – that epitome of the gunboat diplomat – would have approved of the combination of patriotism and paternalism, with a solid (if concealable) base of traditional commercialism. The tiny state of Kuwait, at the head of the Persian (or Arabian) Gulf, was threatened with annexation by her large, powerful and newly-republican neighbour, Iraq. Britain and Kuwait had had friendly relations since 1899 and, since 1948, Britain had had generous concessions on the oil deposits which had been discovered in 1938. The King of Iraq had been overthrown in 1958 and the last British troops had left a year later; Iraq was given regular presents of arms and equipment by an entirely disinterested Soviet Union. On 25 June 1961 President Qassim of Iraq announced his intention of annexing Kuwait forthwith, and the Emir appealed to Britain for help. Quite why the President felt that he could announce his intentions so well in advance of what were going to be unpopular actions is not clear, but his action in so doing allowed Britain to come to Kuwait's assistance without actually having to attack Iraq. The speed of Britain's response was helped by the fact that 42 Commando were

Silver cup, the Inter-Squadron Football Cup. Presented to the Sergeants, the Royal Scots Greys, by Wm. McEwan & Co. Ltd., Edinburgh 1965. *Hallmark: Birmingham 1923-24. Maker: Warren and Bond.*

already en route from the Far East in the carrier *Bulwark*, and so were able to divert to Kuwait, which was reached on 1 July.

The Carabiniers were stationed in Aden at the time, as the duty tank regiment for Middle East operations. This meant that, because of Britain's commitments throughout widely separated parts of the area – especially in the Gulf region, half a squadron of Centurions was kept permanently afloat in the Gulf in either Tank Landing Ships (LSTs) or Tank Landing Craft (LCTs). The crews, and the remainder of the Regiment's tanks, were in Aden, ready to move by air to join their tanks once the LSTs or LCTs had delivered them to wherever trouble had broken out. In addition, in case of emergency, eight Centurions and ammunition were stockpiled in Kuwait. An entire squadron of the Carabiniers, C squadron commanded by Major John Barkworth, was therefore able to deploy in Kuwait, via Bahrein, on 1 July after the airport had been secured by 42 Commando, and while Hawker Hunters of 8 Squadron RAF flew in to provide air support. British forces in Kuwait gradually built up over the next few days, and some units joined the Carabiniers on the Mutla Ridge which lay between the Iraqi border and the airport. There were problems from the intense heat during the alert, the hulls of the Centurions becoming hot enough to fry eggs on and the water in the jerrycans being hot enough to make instant coffee with.

The expected Iraqi attack never materialised and so, by October, British forces were beginning to be withdrawn, the last leaving on the 19th.

When, after this brief period of excitement, the 3rd Carabiniers returned to Europe, it was to return to the alternating duty of BAOR and England. At the end of the 1960s, phase two of the Army cuts having been continued by the Labour Governments of 1963 and 1966, the announcement was made that the Regiment would amalgamate with The Royal Scots Greys (2nd Dragoons) in 1971. In that year the 3rd Carabiniers were stationed in Herford as part of BAOR.

Royal Scots Greys

The Greys had come out of the Second World War with losses of 154 officers and other ranks. Their involvement in action in three theatres of the war was reflected in the award of the Military Cross to twenty-one officers (serving with the Regiment) and in the award of the Military Medal to nineteen other ranks, the good shooting of Sergeant McMeekin gaining him two Military Medal awards.

As post-war demobilisations took their toll, the Regiment settled down for the next seven years as one of the armoured units stationed in the north German plain. To begin with, during 1947, the Regiment was so reduced in strength that its organisation was trimmed to Headquarters squadron and one sabre squadron. The post-war years in Germany necessitated a great deal of bridge-building, in public relations terms, between the German civil population and the forces of occupation, who were only slowly changing from being occupiers to defenders. The organisation of Tattoos and other events, in which the well-known flair of the British Army for spectacle could be demonstrated, aided the process, and the Regiment was able to contribute to a musical ride – with the eight performers from the Greys in full dress and mounted on greys – to the Berlin Tattoo of August 1947.

In addition to its equestrian excellence, demonstrated at Rhine Army horse shows, at Royal Tournaments and in Olympic Games, the Regiment also managed to establish what was to become, in terms of its public face, one of the most well-known aspects of the Greys and its successor regiment: the Pipes and Drums, known at the time as the Pipe Band. A small "pipe band" had existed in pre-war years in India, but its existence was quite unofficial. During the post-war period in Germany, at the end of the 1940s, the Pipes and Drums of the Regiment were officially recognised by the War Office and slowly increased in both size and competence over the next five years. King George VI, the Regiment's Colonel-in-Chief from 1939 until his death in 1952, assisted considerably with its image and granted the Pipes and Drums the right to wear Royal Stewart tartan. In 1951 the official establishment of the Pipes and Drums was a mere six pipers, but there were actually eight pipers, a pipe-major, four side-drummers and a bass drummer. In 1954 the Pipes and Drums were so well advanced that they appeared on parade in full dress alongside the Regimental Band for the visit of the Queen to Tobruk, where the Regiment was stationed. In 1955, their strength at eighteen, the Pipes and Drums made their first television appearance, at the Soldiers', Sailors' and Airmen's Families Association Tattoo at White City stadium in London, and in 1956 they first appeared at the Edinburgh Military Tattoo. Since then they have never looked back.

The Officers of The Royal Scots Greys at dinner on the 150th anniversary of the Battle of Waterloo 1965. The present Colonel of the Regiment, Lieutenant General Sir Norman Arthur KCB, then a major, is seated in the left foreground, at the end of the table. Artist: Robin Guthrie (1902-71).

In April 1952, after a short period in Aldershot, the Regiment was posted to Cyrenaica, its sabre squadrons having received Centurions by that time. Britain's commitments in North Africa and the Middle East have been described above, and it remained necessary for some time to have armoured regiments not only trained to serve in desert conditions but also present in those areas in case of emergencies. The Regiment disembarked from H.M. Troopship *Empire Windrush* (famous two or three years previously for its role in transporting the first mass immigration of West Indians to Britain) at Tobruk in early May 1952 and moved to its station at Barce, fifty-six miles north-east of Benghazi. Over the next two years its three sabre squadrons were detached in turn to serve in either the Suez Canal zone or in Jordan, as political situations demanded, but a detachment of volunteers provided a mounted escort for the Queen on her first visit as Sovereign to Edinburgh in June 1953.

The Queen had become Colonel-in-Chief of the Regiment on 1 June 1953 and visited the Regiment during her State Visit to Libya in 1954. The Greys left Barce in 1955 and returned to Britain, handing over their tanks to 5th Royal Tank Regiment. On arrival in England the Greys squadrons were dispersed, A squadron to Tilshead in Wiltshire, B squadron to Castlemartin in Pembrokeshire,

C squadron to Lulworth in Dorset and HQ squadron to Crookham in Hampshire. The function of the dispersed squadrons, at this period, was to conduct training camps and provide the support of regular soldiers for yeomanry and other Territorial Army units, and this continued until 1956 when the Greys moved to Catterick in Yorkshire.

In 1956 two important ceremonies were held, one in London and the other in Edinburgh; both involved two of the items most significant to the Greys from the point of view of their inextricable association with the Regiment's traditions. The Queen presented the Regiment with a new guidon in July, during her annual visit to Edinburgh, and on the 18th of the previous month (Waterloo Day) the Greys received back from the safe-keeping of the Governor of the Royal Hospital, Chelsea, the eagle and standard of the French 45th Infantry which Ensign Charles Ewart had taken 141 years before. Two days after the new guidon was presented in the grounds of the Palace of Holyroodhouse, on 7 July 1956, the eagle and standard were handed over to the safe-keeping of the Scottish United Services Museum at a ceremony on the esplanade of Edinburgh Castle, opposite the tomb in which Ensign Ewart's remains are buried.

The Regiment remained in Catterick during 1957 and 1958, training recruits for the Royal Armoured Corps, until returning to Germany, to Munster, at the end of that tour of duty in England. After arrival in Germany, recruiting in Scotland was increased in profile, it having been a matter of concern for some years in the Regiment that so few recruits were Scottish, and recruiting-parties operating in Scotland in 1959 and 1960 secured about 100 recruits in both years. The tour in 1961 was accompanied by a Centurion tank and received suitable press coverage. As National Service ended, so the Greys became the first regiment in the Army to achieve an establishment formed entirely of regulars.

Leaving Germany in 1962, the Greys were again dispersed by squadrons. After spending a fortnight in Edinburgh in July, preparing for service in the Middle and Far East, the Regiment moved to Aden, with C squadron joining 48th Gurkha Infantry Brigade in Hong Kong. While stationed in Aden, each of the remaining two sabre squadrons spent rotating tours of duty afloat in the Persian Gulf as part of the Amphibious Warfare Squadron of the Royal Navy; ready for the sort of emergency which had galvanised the Carabiniers in 1961. Between September and December 1962 the Pipes and Drums and Military Band paid a visit to North America, in company with the Argyll and Sutherland Highlanders' Band and Pipes and Drums, and played in sixty-five cities in seventy-eight days in both America and Canada.

In February 1964 the Greys returned to north Germany, to the vast training area at Fallingbostel, between Hamburg and Hanover, and remained stationed

Silver goblet. Presented by the Gordon Highlanders to commemorate our affiliation with The Royal Scots Greys over the years, especially between 1967-1969. *Hallmark: London 1969-70. Maker: Carrington and Company Ltd.*

there until November 1969. In 1965 the 150th anniversary of the Battle of Waterloo was celebrated in Germany, Belgium and in London; principal Regimental celebrations being in Brussels and on the battlefield itself, with four days of sports, games, balls and dinners being held at Fallingbostel.

In 1966 Lieutenant-Colonel John Stanier became Commanding Officer, on transfer from the Queen's Own Hussars. He became Field Marshal Sir John Stanier in 1985 and was Colonel of The Royal Scots Dragoon Guards from 1979 until 1984, having been Chief of the General Staff from 1982 until 1985. As Commanding Officer, Colonel Stanier was involved in the temporary disinterment of Sergeant Ewart's remains from the esplanade of Edinburgh Castle in 1967, an operation made necessary by the rebuilding of the east wall of the esplanade. While the rebuilding was in progress, Ewart's remains rested in the vault of the Callander family at Prestonhall, Major David Callander MC having been an officer in the Regiment between 1939 and 1948, and were reburied on the esplanade in 1968.

The late 1960s were years of considerable disquiet for the Regiment and for the Army as a whole. Publication of the Defence White Paper of 1967 served to underline the unchanging nature of government's commitment to reductions in defence expenditure which had begun, if in a controlled manner, in the late 1950s, and for some time the Regiment's fate was uncertain. For some time in 1967 it seemed likely that the Regiment would be amalgamated with its fellow remaining unamalgamated Dragoon regiment, 1st (Royal) Dragoons, but, so it is reported, the Royals were not keen on this merger – despite the age-old friendship between the regiments – because they feared a Caledonian takeover. Announcement of a reprieve from either amalgamation or disbandment came in November 1967 and was greeted with a corporate sigh of relief, and great celebration, by the Regiment.

The Royals amalgamated in 1969 with The Royal Horse Guards (The Blues) to form The Blues and Royals (Royal Horse Guards and 1st Dragoons). By continuing, and indeed extending, the defence cuts of the 1950s, the Labour Governments of the 1960s were committing themselves to a complete withdrawal from points east of Suez, and from the Gulf Region, by the early 1970s. Despite, however, the likelihood of armoured desert warfare being limited, C and B squadrons of the Regiment trained in Libya in 1965 and 1966 and were followed there for the same purpose by A squadron in 1968.

The celebrations of 1967 did not last long, however, and in February 1969 it became known that the Greys would amalgamate two years later with the 3rd Carabiniers. In the intervening two years, however, the Regiment was active in new roles and places.

In November 1969 the Regiment returned to Edinburgh, for the first time in thirty years, and converted from tanks to various marques of armoured cars, becoming an armoured reconnaissance regiment with an airportable function. Its troop of helicopters, which it had had since 1965, was expanded to a squadron strength of six, and – during the eighteen-month home tour – it was to separate its other squadrons between a variety of locations.

At the end of 1969 B Squadron, its conversion to Ferret scoutcars complete, left to join a United Nations peace-keeping force in Cyprus, based at Zyyi Camp. Early in 1970 C squadron completed its conversion to Ferrets, a change which involved them also training for service in the airportable role, and A squadron finished converting to Saladin armoured cars. While the sections of the Regiment remaining in Scotland suffered cold weather and an even more than usually prolonged winter, during which training took place at Otterburn in Northumberland (an area renowned for its gentle climate and perpetually fine weather), B squadron roughed it in Cyprus, earning their United Nations medals by learning to water-ski, scuba-dive and free-fall parachute jump. B squadron returned exhausted from Cyprus in June 1970 and C squadron had to be bullied into replacing them. A squadron were destined for Sharjah in the Persian Gulf in July, where they collaborated in exercises with the Scots Guards and Trucial Oman Scouts. In July 1970 B squadron were ordered to Northern Ireland at three days' notice, but spent only ten days in what was becoming one of Britain's newest trouble spots before being recalled. They were replaced in February 1971 by C squadron, commanded by HRH the Duke of Kent, which had returned from Cyprus in December 1970, and which returned to the mainland from Northern Ireland a month after arriving.

Although operational and training duties continued, the thoughts of most of the Regiment must have been on the ceremonies of amalgamation which were to take place in July 1971.

HRH the Duke of Kent, 1978. Prince Edward, Duke of Kent, was commissioned into The Royal Scots Greys in 1955 and commanded C squadron from 1970 until 1971. He left the Regiment in 1976. He is depicted in regimental No. 1 dress, with the sash of a Knight Grand Cross of the Order of St Michael and St George, the Stars of a Knight Grand Cross of the Order of St Michael and St George and of the Royal Victorian Order, and the neck Badge of Grand Master of the Order of St Michael and St George. His aiguillette signifies the appointment of Aide-de-Camp to the Queen. Artist: Madeleine Rampling (1941-).

The Royal Scots Dragoon Guards (Carabiniers and Greys)

The year 1971 was, aside from the years on active service, a year of particularly frantic action and great reward. All the battles that could be fought to attempt to prevent amalgamation had been fought, outside the Regiments principally and fortunately, several years before. While there was undoubted sadness, both at the disappearance of the last unamalgamated cavalry regiment and at the further amalgamation of the Carabiniers, this sadness was – in the Regiments at least – tinged with optimism for the future and a determination to make the amalgamation work.

As with the amalgamation which created the 3rd Carabiniers in 1922, it was felt important to retain characteristics of both Regiments once they had become one. Since the new Regiment was to be a regiment of Dragoon Guards, it would have to have a standard and not a guidon, and this most precious of all Regimental

Ram's head table snuff mull. Presented by Lieutenant-Colonel A.M. Sprot, Royal Scots Greys 1941-62, and Major G.H.C. Sprot, 3rd Carabiniers 1941-46, 2nd July 1971. To Lieutenant-Colonel A.J. Bateman, Officers, Warrant Officers, Non-Commissioned Officers and Other Ranks, The Royal Scots Dragoon Guards (Carabiniers and Greys).

possessions could be used to perpetuate the memory of all three of its predecessors. The uniqueness of the Greys' bearskin cap and their "vandyked" (zig-zag) pattern forage-cap band would be retained, but the collars and cuffs of the full-dress tunic would change from Greys' blue to Carabiniers' yellow. Their overall trousers would retain the Carabiniers' double narrow seam stripe, but in Greys' yellow, not Carabiniers' white. There would be new badges and buttons, the Waterloo eagle of the Greys superimposed upon the crossed carbines of the Carabiniers. The badge of the Prince of Wales' plumes, coronet and motto would be worn as a sleeve badge. As may be surmised, the changes in uniform were most noticeable on the occasions when full dress was worn, and the Military Band were the most habitual wearers of that.

There was little chance of the amalgamation going unnoticed in Scotland, so extensive was the press treatment of the preparations for it, the battles against it and the ceremony itself. What sealed the name of the new Regiment in the minds of a public, who would have been hard put to tell one regiment from another, was the immense, and almost overnight, success of a record released by the Pipes and Drums and Military Band shortly after amalgamation, *Amazing Grace*. Initially recorded as part of a long-playing disc, *Farewell to the Greys*, it became increasingly popular during 1972 and was then released as a single, whereupon sales took off. It became top of the popular music "charts" in Britain – a position that it occupied for five weeks – and in Canada, South Africa, Australia and New Zealand. By the end of 1972 *Amazing Grace* had sold four million copies worldwide and the BBC named it the bestselling record of 1972.

The week of amalgamation ceremonies and rehearsals took place in Edinburgh during the end of June and beginning of July 1971. At the end of June the Queen

4 gold discs awarded to The Royal Scots Dragoon Guards to mark the sales of their record Amazing Grace.
Top, left: From NZFPI 1974.
Top, right: For 1 million copies sold worldwide, from RCA.
Bottom left: For over 20,000 copies sold in New Zealand 1973.
Bottom right: For achieving a South African gold record.

presented the Regiment which was to be formed on 2 July with a drum horse, *Trojan*. The ceremony on 2 July began with the disbandment of the Greys and Carabiniers, whereupon the Greys' guidon and Carabiniers' standard were marched off. This was followed by the formation of The Royal Scots Dragoon Guards, whereupon the new standard was consecrated, presented to the Regiment by its Colonel-in-Chief and then trooped. The Greys' guidon was subsequently laid up in the Scottish National War Memorial in Edinburgh Castle and the Carabiniers' standard in Chester Cathedral.

Following amalgamation, the Regiment moved back to Herford in BAOR, where the Carabiniers had been stationed, but the newly-created D squadron undertook a short tour of peace-keeping duties in Northern Ireland almost immediately. For the remainder of 1971, and into 1972, the Regiment was divided between Herford and Northern Ireland, squadrons swapping places as tours of duty ended. During 1972 the Regiment's peace-keeping role continued; B squadron in Northern Ireland and D squadron in Cyprus. At the end of 1972 training began for the Regiment to convert to the Chieftain Main Battle Tank, and in May 1973 a move was undertaken to Osnabrück from Herford. Later in the same year the sub-Home Headquarters in Chester, where Home Headquarters 3rd Carabiniers had been since 1959, was relinquished and the Home Headquarters of the Regiment was fixed at Edinburgh Castle. D squadron remained detached from the main body of the Regiment during 1973, doing a tour in Northern Ireland as an armoured reconnaissance squadron between June and October, and remained in Scotland where they represented the Scottish face of the Regiment, so vital for ensuring that recruits continued to be attracted.

The Regiment has been many things in its more than three hundred years of existence, but not for a long time had it served as foot-soldiers pure and simple.

Items of full dress uniform of The Royal Scots Dragoon Guards depicted by Paul Maze, an artist who served briefly with the Royal Scots Greys as an interpreter in 1914. A gift from the artist to commemorate the tercentenary, 1978. Artist: Paul Maze (1887-1979).

However, it is perhaps a measure both of its versatility and of the exigencies of the situation in Northern Ireland in 1974 that, for nearly four months – between the beginning of May and the end of August – that was the role played by Scotland's regular cavalry. Occupied in the role of prison warders around the Maze prison and as infantrymen elsewhere in the province, the Regiment arrived just as the Protestant Loyalist Ulster Defence Association was feeling at its strongest, and as the Ulster Workers' Council was about to organise a power-workers' strike throughout Northern Ireland. No casualties resulted from this tour of duty in an unfamiliar role.

1975 was spent in retraining after the brief infantry experience. B squadron had moved to Suffield in Canada immediately after returning from Northern Ireland in September 1974 and were able to report favourably on the training and firing possibilities of the vast expanses of the Canadian training area. A major exercise involving Regimental Headquarters and A and C squadrons was run at Suffield in August, and the majority of the Regiment returned to Osnabrück in September to be occupied in BAOR exercises.

A further tour of duty in Northern Ireland followed between May and August 1976, and in the following year the Regiment was widely dispersed between Germany and Catterick, with a troop in Northern Ireland and another in Belize. Its "aid to the civil power" role was revived too, during the firemen's strike of 1977 when it performed fire-fighting duties in northern England and Scotland.

1978 was the tercentenary year of the Regiment's existence, measured from the raising of the original three troops of dragoons in Scotland in 1678. It was celebrated in fine style, with a tank parade down Princes Street in Edinburgh, the

Silver model of a Chieftain Main Battle Tank. The property of the Corporals' Mess, The Royal Scots Dragoon Guards (Carabiniers & Greys). Hallmark: Sheffield 1982-83. Maker: Jack Spencer Goldsmiths.

Piece of Tyrone crystal, presented to The Royal Scots Dragoon Guards by the Royal Ulster Constabulary and Ulster Defence Regiment, Dungannon 1976, to commemorate the tercentary of the Royal Scots Greys 1978.

salute being taken by HRH the Duke of Kent. This was followed by a parade in Holyrood Park attended by the Regiment's Colonel-in-Chief, HM The Queen. Later in the same year the Regiment attended the Edinburgh Military Tattoo in some strength.

During 1979 the Regiment moved back to Germany, to Athlone Barracks in the giant Sennelager training complex, and recaptured B squadron from Berlin and its troop from Belize. Between September and November 1980 the infantry role was again called for, as the Regiment was organised into two squadrons, equipped as foot soldiers, to patrol the city centre and Ardoyne area of Belfast. In 1981 the Suffield area of Canada was again occupied for training and firing practice, and exercises in Germany characterised the remainder of the year. The Regiment continued to be equipped with Chieftain tanks during its time in Germany, but in 1982 these were becoming increasingly fitted with the Improved Fire Control System (IFCS) which allowed, in theory, far more accurate and far faster shooting than hitherto. Conversion to this new system, which would become standard on all Chieftains in order to improve their firing capabilities, occupied most of the Regiment for much of the year.

The Regiment completed its most recent tour of duty in Sennelager in October 1986, the previous eight years in Germany having firmly established it as one of the British Army's crack armoured regiments. It arrived in Tidworth, in Hampshire, for a two-year stay, at the beginning of November 1986, and will

Field Marshal Sir John Stanier GCB MBE 1986. Sir John Stanier transferred to The Royal Scots Greys as Commanding Officer in 1966 from the Queen's Own Hussars and commanded the Regiment until 1968. He was Colonel of The Royal Scots Dragoon Guards from 1979 to 1984 and was Chief of the General Staff from 1982 to 1985, being promoted to Field Marshal in 1985. He is depicted, in the Cavalry and Guards Club, in a Field Marshal's frock coat beneath the Mantle and Collar of a Knight Grand Cross of the Order of the Bath. Artist: Edward Hall (1922-   ).

return to BAOR, to Fallingbostel, in November 1988, to convert to the newest Main Battle Tank of the Army, Challenger.

If the years since the end of the Second World War have seemed devoid of the excitement that retelling the stories of active service may provide, it should be remembered that the modern Army provides a species of excitement denied to many officers, and most other ranks, in previous years of its existence. That the British Army has not had to go, en masse, on active service since 1945 is because, amongst other things, it is so well-trained and so professional that these factors provide a good reason for not taking it on. Not that the Army, or the Regiment of which this résumé is barely a history, is at all complacent about its capacity to carry all before it, should the unthinkable happen. Its lack of complacency results in its constant training, constant striving for efficiency, for perfection, for excellence. Yet it still maintains that sense of proportion, even of the ridiculous, which makes the British Army, and certainly its élite regiments, the envy of nations far richer, with far larger military forces.

The Royal Scots Dragoon Guards (Carabiniers & Greys) is one among many regiments of the British Royal Armoured Corps which nurses and nurtures its traditions, its values and its record jealously. In believing that it is second to none, it does not denigrate the professionalism of its fellows, but merely states its own attitude to its profession. This professionalism has made it, and its three predecessors, a Regiment, and Regiments, which generations of soldiers, of all ranks, have wished to join. That so many of these have come from the same families is indicative of the largely unspoken emotion that a "family" regiment inspires, and of the loyalty and service it produces. There can be little doubt that the Regiment's unbroken connection with Scotland, where soldiering has never ceased to be an honourable profession, contributes largely to this, and even those soldiers who detest bagpipes and loathe horses would subscribe to the indefinably powerful glamour that this irresistible combination produces. Soldiering today is no less messy and sordid a business than it has ever been, allowing for many comparative changes in standards, weapons and sensibilities over the past three centuries. It remains, for the majority of civilians, a job which someone else has to do, which is often misunderstood, frequently criticised and rarely given thanks for. That regiments like The Royal Scots Dragoon Guards can do it so well, concealing a large degree of professionalism beneath an elegant veneer of style and panache, contributes considerably not only to what was once recognised as "the cavalry spirit", but also to the excellence which many civilians take too easily for granted.

The Regiment whose history you have just read is now 310 years old. In the absence of a nuclear cataclysm, which it is its job to help avoid, we should hope that it will continue to set standards and achieve those performances which have contributed to its position as one of the British Army's most famous and most respected regiments. Regiments make history every day, and they rely both on their traditions and their training to maintain the standards by which they measure themselves. The finest traditions of The Royal Scots Dragoons Guards (Carabiniers & Greys) are second to none in the British Army.

SUGGESTIONS FOR FURTHER READING

GENERAL

Anglesey, Marquess of, *A History of the British Cavalry*, 4 volumes (London, Leo Cooper, 1973-86)

Brereton, John M., *The Horse in War* (Newton Abbot, David & Charles, 1976)

Fortescue, J.W., *History of the British Army*, 13 volumes (London, Macmillan, 1899-1930)

Guy, Alan J., *Oeconomy and Discipline: Officership and Administration in the British Army, 1714-1763* (Manchester, Manchester University Press, 1985)

Harries-Jenkins, Gwyn, *The Army in Victorian Society* (London, Routledge & Kegan Paul, 1977)

Macksey, Kenneth, *A History of the Royal Armoured Corps, 1914-1975* (Beaminster, Newtown Publications, 1983)

Skelley, Alan Ramsay, *The Victorian Army at Home* (London, Croom Helm, 1977)

Spiers, Edward M., *The Army and Society, 1815-1914* (London, Longman, 1980)

Strachan, Hew, *From Waterloo to Balaclava: Tactics, Technology and the British Army, 1815-1854* (Cambridge, Cambridge University Press, 1985)

Strachan, Hew, *Wellington's Legacy: The Reform of the British Army, 1830-1854* (Manchester, Manchester University Press, 1984)

Teichman, Oskar, "Yeomanry as an Aid to Civil Power, 1795-1867", *Journal of the Society for Army Historical Research* 1940, vol. 19, 75-91, 127-143

UNIFORM

Carman, W.Y., *British Military Uniforms from Contemporary Pictures: Henry VII to the Present Day* (London, Leonard Hill, 1957)

Carman, W.Y., *Richard Simkin's Uniforms of the British Army: The Cavalry Regiments* (Exeter, Webb & Bower, 1982)

Chappell, Mike, *British Cavalry Equipments, 1800-1941* (London, Osprey, 1981)

Fosten, Bryan, *Wellington's Heavy Cavalry*, (London, Osprey, 1982)

Strachan, Hew, *British Military Uniforms, 1768-1796: The Dress of the British Army from Official Sources* (London, Arms & Armour Press, 1975)

REGIMENTAL HISTORIES

3rd Dragoon Guards

Anonymous, *3rd Carabiniers (Prince of Wales's Dragoon Guards): 250th Anniversary of the Raising of the 3rd Dragoon Guards (Prince of Wales's) and The Carabiniers (6th Dragoon Guards)* (Aldershot, Gale & Polden, 1935)

Cannon, Richard, *Historical Record of The Third, or Prince of Wales' Regiment of Dragoon Guards* (London, Wm. Clowes, 1838)

Holt, H.P., *The History of The Third (Prince of Wales's) Dragoon Guards, 1914-1918* (Guildford, Billing, 1937)

Oatts, Lewis, *I Serve: Regimental History of the 3rd Carabiniers* (Chester, the Regiment, 1966)

6th Dragoon Guards

Cannon, Richard, *Historical Record of The Sixth Regiment of Dragoon Guards, or The Carabineers* (London, Longman, Orme, 1839)

Sixth Dragoon Guards, *War Diary of 'A' Squadron 6th Dragoon Guards (Carabiniers), August–December 1914* (Eastbourne, the Regiment, n.d.)

Sprot, A., *A Continuation of the Historical Records of the VI D.G. Carabineers* (Chatham, Gale & Polden, 1888)

2nd Dragoons

Almack, Edward, *The History of the Second Dragoons: Royal Scots Greys* (London, Alexander Moring, 1908)

Balfour Paul, Sir James, *The 2nd Dragoons: Royal Scots Greys* (Glasgow, James Maclehose, 1919)

Cannon, Richard, *Historical Record of The Royal Regiment of Scots Dragoons, now The Second or Royal North British Dragoons, commonly called The Scots Greys* (London, Longman, Orme 1840)

Blacklock, Michael, *The Royal Scots Greys* (London, Leo Cooper, 1971)

Carver, R.M.P., *Second to None: the Royal Scots Greys, 1919–1945* (Glasgow, the Regiment, 1954)

Groves, Percy, *History of the 2nd Dragoons The Royal Scots Greys, 1678–1893* (Edinburgh, W. & A.K. Johnstone, 1893)

Hay, Lord John, "The Royal Regiment of Scots Dragoons (Now the Scots Greys) Two Hundred Years Ago, Being Letters by Colonel Lord John Hay: with notes by Edward Rodger", *Scottish Historical Review* 1917, vol. 14, 216–237

Pomeroy, Ralph, *et al*, *History of The Royal Scots Greys (The Second Dragoons) August 1914–March 1919* (S.l., s.n., 1932)

Somerville, Alexander, *The Autobiography of a Working Man*, Edited with an Introduction by John Carswell (London, Turnstile Press, 1951)

CAMPAIGN HISTORIES

Baynes, John, *The Jacobite Rising of 1715* (London, Cassell, 1970)

Buchanan, George, *Letters from an Officer of the Scots Greys to his Mother during the Crimean War* (London, Rivingstons, 1866)

Carver, Michael, *Dilemmas of the Desert War: a new look at the Libyan Campaign, 1940–1942* (London, Batsford, 1986)

Carver, Michael, *El Alamein* (London, Batsford, 1962)

Chamberlain, Peter, and **Ellis**, Chris, *British and American Tanks of World War II* (London, Arms & Armour Press, 1969)

Dewar, Michael, *The British Army in Northern Ireland* (London, Arms & Armour Press, 1985)

Dewar, Michael, *Brush Fire Wars: Minor Campaigns of the British Army since 1945* (London, R. Hale, 1984)

Dunstan, Simon, *Tank War Korea* (London, Arms & Armour Press, 1985)

Edwardes, Michael, *Battles of the Indian Mutiny* (London, Batsford, 1963)

Emery, Frank, *Marching Over Africa: Letters from Victorian Soldiers* (London, Hodder & Stoughton, 1986)

Evans, Sir Geoffrey, and **Brett-James**, Anthony, *Imphal: A Flower on Lofty Heights* (London, Macmillan, 1962)

Fenton, Thomas C., "The Peninsula and Waterloo Letters of Captain Thomas C. Fenton (Scots Greys): edited by C.W. de fforde," *Journal of the Society for Army Historical Research* 1975, vol.53, 210–231

Fraser, David, *And We Shall Shock Them: the British Army in the Second World War* (London, Hodder & Stoughton, 1983)

Gates, David, *The Spanish Ulcer: a History of the Peninsular War* (London, Allen & Unwin, 1986)

Glover, Michael, *The Peninsular War, 1807-1814* (Newton Abbot, David & Charles, 1974)

Goldmann, Charles S., *With General French and the Cavalry in South Africa* (London, Macmillan, 1902)

Hamill, Desmond, *Pig in the Middle: the Army in Northern Ireland* (London, Methuen, 1985)

Howarth, David, *A Near Run Thing: the Day of Waterloo* (London, Collins, 1968)

Jackson, William, *Withdrawal From Empire: a Military View* (London, Batsford, 1986)

Johnston, Sergeant, "A Waterloo Journal (Scots Greys)" edited by Christopher T. Atkinson, *Journal of the Society for Army Historical Research* 1960 vol. 38, 29-42

Kemp, Anthony, *Weapons and Equipment of the Marlborough Wars* (Poole, Blandford, 1980)

Keown-Boyd, Henry, *A Good Dusting: a Centenary Review of the Sudan Campaigns 1883-1899* (London, Leo Cooper, 1986)

Kinglake, A.W., *The Invasion of the Crimea* 6 volumes (Edinburgh, Blackwood, 1877)

Linklater, Eric, *The Campaign in Italy* (London, H.M.S.O., 1951)

Lucas Phillips, C.E., *Alamein* (London, Heinemann, 1962)

Montgomery, Field Marshal, *Normandy to the Baltic* (London, Hutchinson, 1947)

North, John, *North-West Europe, 1944-5: the Achievement of 21st Army Group* (London, H.M.S.O., 1953)

Pakenham, Thomas, *The Boer War* (London, Weidenfeld & Nicolson, 1979)

Pemberton, W. Baring, *Battles of the Crimean War* (London, Batsford, 1962)

Robson, Brian, *The Road to Kabul: the Second Afghan War, 1878-1881* (London, Arms & Armour Press, 1986)

Shepperd, G.A., *The Italian Campaign, 1943-45* (London, Arthur Barker, 1968)

Slim, Field Marshal, *Defeat into Victory* (London, Cassell, 1956)

Sutherland, John P., *Men of Waterloo* (London, Muller, 1967)

Vaughan-Thomas, Wynford, *Anzio* (London, Longman, 1961)

Weller, Jac, *Wellington at Waterloo* (London, Longmans, Green, 1967)

Wood, Sir Evelyn, *Cavalry in the Waterloo Campaign* (London, Sampson Low, Marston, 1895)

BIOGRAPHIES

Anonymous, *A Memoir of Brigadier General Walter Long (of the Scots Greys)* (London, John Murray, 1921)

Bonham Carter, Victor, *Soldier True: Life and Times of Field-Marshal Sir William Robertson, 1860-1933* (London, 1963)

Cloake, John, *Templer: Tiger of Malaya* (London, Harrap, 1985)

Davies, Christian, *The Life and Adventures of Mrs Christian Davies, Commonly Called Mother Ross* (London, 1740)

Dunfermline, James Abercromby, Lord, *Lieutenant General Sir Ralph Abercromby KB, 1793-1801: A Memoir by his Son* (Edinburgh, Edmonston & Douglas, 1861)

Holmes, Richard, *The Little Field Marshal: Sir John French* (London, Cape, 1981)

Keyes, Elizabeth, *Geoffrey Keyes* (London, Newnes, 1956)

Maze, Paul, *A Frenchman in Khaki* (London, Heinemann, 1934)

Ramsay, Balcarres D.W., *Rough Recollections of Military Service and Society* 2 Volumes (Edinburgh, Blackwood, 1882)

Robertson, Sir William, *From Private to Field-Marshal: Autobiography* (London, Constable, 1921)

INDEX